HOW
CAN
TEACHERS
INTEGRATE

Critical Thinking

IN
THEIR
STUDENTS?

Muhammad Jamil

Abstract

Critical thinking has been given much importance to the progress of twenty-first-century learners in national and international education policy documents as well as in theoretical literature on secondary science education. The current study aimed to develop an understanding of how science teachers interpret and enact education policy recommendations for developing critical thinking skills among secondary school students in public schools. The study in hand was a qualitative research with a multiple case study design. A purposive sampling technique was used to select four public secondary schools as research sites. From each school, three science teachers teaching the subjects of Physics, Chemistry or Biology were selected, which comprised 12 participants for the study. This qualitative study was done in different phases to address the research objectives. In the first phase, the education policy documents (National Education Policy 2009 & National Curriculum of Grades IX-X for Physics, Chemistry and Biology, 2006) were analyzed to understand policy recommendations regarding the development of critical thinking skills. In the second phase, teacher interpretations of the policy documents' recommendations were explored through a self-developed semi-structured interview guide keeping in view the objectives of the study, guidelines from previous literature and the opinion of education experts. In the third phase, classroom observations were conducted to find out the participant teachers' practices in a natural context related to the development of critical thinking skills. All teachers were observed six times while teaching their subjects. Video recordings were made for their observations in the classrooms and reflective field notes were also prepared for further analysis of the observational data. Qualitative content analysis with the facilitation of *Nvivo* 11 was used to analyse data from documents, interviews, video recordings and field notes. Findings suggested that critical thinking was emphasised in all the education policy documents analysed for this study. Different pedagogical practices like questioning, discussions, debates and cooperative learning were suggested to be used. In assessment, questions related to critical thinking were also suggested to be included. Analysis of interview data revealed that teachers had little awareness of the term 'critical thinking' and its implication in the classrooms. The teachers were mostly using the lecture method with some other pedagogical practices, but their main focus was not to develop critical thinking skills rather than to pass the students in the exam. They used most of the teaching methods near exams. Moreover, analysis of classroom observations revealed that most of the teachers used the lecture method with different pedagogical practices like questioning, discussion, diagramming and use of the whiteboard as visual aid. In almost all the observations, the main focus of the teachers was to cover the content in the given time period, and there was not much focus on developing critical thinking skills. It is suggested that teachers should use different pedagogical practices like questioning, cooperative learning, discussions, debates, collaborative learning and students' engagement for the development of critical thinking skills among students, as prescribed in the education policy documents. The study recommends a top-down change to implement the policies in the educational institutions. Assessment of students should also be revised with its focus on the development of critical thinking skills.

Keywords: Critical thinking, education policy documents, pedagogy, science teachers

Dedication

To

My lovely Teachers & Parents

Table of Contents

Abstract v

Dedication ix

List of Tables xvi

List of Figures xvii

Glossary xviii

CHAPTER 1 1

Introduction 1

Background of the Study 1

Statement of the Problem 4

Aim of the Study 5

Objectives of the Study 5

Research Questions 5

Significance of the Study 6

Conceptual Framework of the Study 8

Some Key Terms 9

    Science Teachers 9

    Critical Thinking Skills 9

    Pedagogy 9

    Education Policy Documents 9

    Practices 10

Delimitations of the Study 10

The Structure of the Dissertation 11

CHAPTER 2 13

Review of the Related Literature 13

Introduction of the Chapter 13

What is Thinking? 13

What is Critical Thinking? 14

Critical Thinking in Different Perspectives 16

History of Critical Thinking 19

Critical Thinking and Delphi Study 22

Critical Thinking Skills 22

Critical Thinking and other kinds of Thinking 26

    Scientific Thinking 26

    Creative Thinking 26

    Reflective Thinking 28

Bloom's Taxonomy and Critical Thinking 29

    Knowledge 30

    Comprehension 30

    Application 31

    Analysis 31

    Synthesis 31

    Evaluation 32

Importance of Critical Thinking 32

    Importance of CT in Education and Teaching 33

    Importance of Critical Thinking in Science Education 35

How to Teach Critical Thinking? 41

Pedagogy for Critical Thinking 47

Pedagogical Practices for Developing Critical Thinking Skills 47

    Cooperative Learning 48

    Collaborative Learning 51

    Questioning 51

Inquiry-based teaching/learning..54

Debates...57

Discussion..57

Problem-solving/Problem based Learning...58

Active Learning 61

Combined Strategies (Questioning, Discussion, Practical work, Dialogue, Problem solving, Examples & Monitoring) 61

Conceptual Framework of the Study 62

Critical Thinking Studies in Pakistani Context...65

Gaps in CT Skills Development Research in Science Students..69

Summary of the Chapter 71

CHAPTER 3 73

Research Methodology 73

Introduction of the Chapter..73

Purpose of Research and Research Questions 73

Research Design 74

Sampling...77

Sampling of Education Policy Documents 77

Research Sites...78

Sampling of Teachers 79

Methods for Data Collection..81

Document Analysis..82

Teachers' Semi-Structured Interviews..83

Classroom Observations 84

Methods of Data Analysis..86

Qualitative Content Analysis of Education Policy Documents 87

Qualitative Content Analysis of Semi-Structured Interviews..89

Qualitative Content Analysis of Classroom Observations..91

Ethical Consideration...92

Procedures for Adopting Trustworthiness 93

Credibility 94

Dependability 96

Transferability 97

CHAPTER 4 98

Data Analysis and Interpretation 98

Introduction of the Chapter 98

Section I. Analysis of Education Policy Documents 99

Introduction about Education Policy Documents 100

Aim of Education/Curriculum and SLOs 101

Importance of CT 105

Pedagogical Practices for Developing CT Skills 107

Assessment and CT 110

Summary: Education Policy Documents Analysis 111

Section 2: Analysis of Semi-Structured Interviews 113

Perceptions about Critical Thinking 115

Importance of CT Perceived by the Participants 117

Focus/Encouragement & Training by the Education Department for CT Skills
Development 122

Pedagogical Practice used by Teachers in the classroom 125

Assessment System regarding CT Skills and Suggestions 129

Barriers in developing CT skills 132

Summary: Analysis of Semi-Structured Interviews 134

Section 3: Classroom Observations 136

Classroom atmosphere 141

Teachers' interaction/engagement in the classroom 144

The focus of the study/explanation of different concepts 149

Pedagogical practices used in the classroom (Methods of teaching, use of audio-visual aids,
asking questions, problem-solving skills, cooperative learning) 154

Summary: Analysis of Classroom Observations 157

CHAPTER 5 159

Findings, Discussion and Recommendations.. 159

Introduction and Overview of the Study... 159

Findings 160

Four Education Policy Documents Recommendations regarding Pedagogy for the
Development of CT Skills 161

Perceptions of Secondary Level Science Teachers regarding Pedagogy for the
Development of CT Skills. 166

Teachers' Practices for Developing CT Skills 170

Discussion of the Results 172

Analysis of Research Question 1: Education Policy Documents Analysis....................... 172

Analysis of Research Question 2: Teachers' Perceptions about Pedagogy for CT Skills
Development... 175

Analysis of research question 3: Teachers' practices for developing CT skills................ 179

Analysis of Research Question 4: Gaps between Policy and Practice.............................. 182

Implications for Policy, Practice and Future Research 185

Implications for Policy... 185

Implications for Practice 188

Implications for Future Research.. 193

References.. 198

Appendix A: Interview Guide... 220

List of Tables

Table 3.1: Demographic Information of Study Participants 81

Table 3.2: Nodes and child nodes used for Document Analysis in Nvivo 89

Table 3.3: Nodes and child nodes used for Interviews data Analysis in Nvivo 91

Table 4.1: Physics Teacher 01 Observation Schedule 137

Table 4.2: Physics Teacher 02 Observation Schedule 137

Table 4.3: Physics Teacher 03 Observation Schedule 137

Table 4.4: Physics Teacher 04 Observation Schedule 138

Table 4.5: Chemistry Teacher 01 Observation Schedule 138

Table 4.6: Chemistry Teacher 02 Observation Schedule 138

Table 4.7: Chemistry Teacher 03 Observation Schedule 139

Table 4.8: Chemistry Teacher 04 Observation Schedule 139

Table 4.9: Biology Teacher 01 Observation Schedule 139

Table 4.10: Biology Teacher 02 Observation Schedule 140

Table 4.11: Biology Teacher 03 Observation Schedule 140

Table 4.12: Biology Teacher 04 Observation Schedule 140

List of Figures

Figure 1. 1. An Action-based framework for analysing teaching 9

Figure 3.1: Data collection process for the current study 82

Figure 3. 2. Nodes and child nodes in Nvivo 11 for data analysis 88

Figure 3.3: Nodes and child nodes in Nvivo 11 for data analysis 90

Figure 4.1: Nodes and Child nodes in Nvivo regarding policy analysis 100

Figure 4.2: Nodes and Child nodes regarding Semi-structured interviews analysis . 114

Figure 5.1: Results of analysis of different aspects regarding CT skills development

.... 160

Figure 5.2: Analysis results of education policy documents' recommendations

regarding pedagogy for developing CT skills 162

Figure 5.3: Analysis and results of teachers' perceptions regarding pedagogy for

developing CT skills 167

Figure 5.4: Analysis of results of the teachers' practices regarding pedagogy for

developing CT skills 171

Glossary

	Abbreviation/ Acronym	Description
•	SLOs	Students Learning Outcomes
•	CT	Critical Thinking
•	NEP	National Education Policy
•	NC	National Curriculum
•	NCB	National Curriculum for Biology, Grades, IX-X
•	NCP	National Curriculum for Physics, Grades, IX-X
•	NCC	National Curriculum for Chemistry, Grades, IX-X
•	QAED	Quaid-e-Azam Academy for Educational Development
•	IER	Institute of Education and Research
•	AIOU	Allama Iqbal Open University
•	UE	University of Education
•	BEd	Bachelor in Education
•	MEd	Master in Education
•	LOTS	Lower-order Thinking Skills
•	HOTS	Higher-order Thinking Skills
•	ADE	Associate Diploma in Education
•	PCTB	Punjab Curriculum and Textbook Board
•	DSD	Directorate of Staff Development
•	SSE	Secondary School Educator
•	BISE	Board of Intermediate and Secondary Education

CHAPTER 1

Introduction

Background of the Study

In this global era, it seems that the main purpose of science education has shifted to developing critical thinking (CT) among students so that they can deal effectively in all spheres of life and it is listed as one of the most important skill of the twenty-first century (Bialik & Fadel, 2015; Wagner, 2014). This skill is deemed essential for becoming reflective thinkers (Higgins, 2015) because of its importance in every sphere of life, including information, technology, economics and politics (Bailey & Mentz, 2015). During the age of 'knowledge explosion', there is a need to discern the information critically to make its use effective (Zhang & Kim, 2018). CT is also necessary for learning and thinking about information as it has become an integral part of growth and development, thus leading towards better competency and higher academic success of the learners (Bialik & Fadel, 2015; Kules, 2016). In addition, critical thinking is now considered essential for students and overall educational outcomes by different researchers (Spatariu, Winsor, Simpson, & Hosman, 2016).

CT has been defined differently in literature for a long time. Socrates defined it as reflective thinking 2500 years ago. In the view of Facione (1990), a committee of experts defined it as purposeful, judgmental and self-regulatory thinking. It has been described as a central point of education with vehicle to educate the human minds (Dewey, 2004; Paul & Elder, 2006a), logical, meaningful, self-regulated, goal-oriented learning with inference, interpretation, analysis, synthesis, evaluation and decision-making skills (Cottrell, 2011; Facione, 2007; Fahim & Pezeshki, 2012; Halx & Reybold, 2006; Mendelman, 2007) and logical conclusions and problem-solving

(Garner, Pugh, & Kaplan, 2016). The last three stages of Bloom's taxonomy (analysis, synthesis and evaluation) are called higher-order thinking skills (Zhao, Pandian, & Singh, 2016). In literature, the most used definition of CT is "The art of analysing and evaluating thinking" (Paul & Elder, 2006a, p. 88).

In science education too, there is focus on CT and is considered as the most important aspect of science education (Demir, 2015; Osborne, 2014). In the view of Yacoubian (2015), critical thinking is the pillar of science education for fostering scientific knowledge in the future citizens. CT has its positive role in different aspects of science education and it plays an important role in the identification of the problems, observations, questioning, exploration, research, decision making, argumentation, discussion, evaluation and solution of problems (Santos, 2017), rejection of arguments (Brown & Ganguly, 2003), the practice of debate, discussion, evaluation and rigorous testing (Osborne, 2014) and problem-solving (Demir, 2015).

Moreover, it is argued that the teaching-learning process should involve critical thinking as it is useful in the general and academic life of an individual (Dwyer, Hogan, & Stewart, 2011) and may serve for the guidance of learners to find solutions to their social problems. Within an informative society, learners should get knowledge and ability to compare and evaluate the knowledge critically with their understanding. However, rote memorisation is a big hindrance in the production of well-rounded knowledge and critically thinking skills in the students.

In international literature, different techniques have been described for the development of CT skills such as observation, argumentation, evaluation, students' engagement and inquiry-based learning (Duran & Dökme, 2016), discussion, group activities, collaboration, self-evaluation, role-playing, simulation, presentations and technology (Osborne, 2014; Savich, 2009; Tok, 2012), explicit instruction, engaged pedagogy, questioning, inquiry and project-based methods (Hooks, 2010; Orlich, Harder, Callahan, Trevisan, & Brown, 2012), cooperative/collaborative learning, conversation, interaction, debates and problem-solving (Fung, 2014; Osborne, 2014).

In Pakistan, the education policy documents, that is, the National Education Policy (NEP, 2009) and the National Curriculum (NC, 2006) regarding science subjects (Physics, Chemistry and Biology) focus on developing CT skills among the secondary school science students. These documents suggest the cultivation of CT skills among students to produce useful citizens, who can effectively face the challenges of the world. In these documents, there are different suggested pedagogical practices for CT skills development among secondary science students like student-centred pedagogies, inquiry based teaching, problem-solving and team-work (NEP, 2009), questioning, problem-solving, discussion, cooperative learning, debates and students' involvement (NCP, 2006), student-centred, activity-based, interactive, participative practical, laboratory work, group-work, inquiry-based, diagrams, flowcharts, graphs, fieldwork and inquiry-based approaches (NCC, 2006), group work, team-setting, formulation of questions, audio-video presentation, diagrams, graphs, flowcharts, demonstration, investigation, debates and drawing (NCB, 2006).

The above discussion shows the interest of CT in international and national context regarding science education. Most of the Pakistani education policy documents focus on producing independent and critical thinking students. Despite given the importance by education policy documents, the performance of the students on questions related to CT is low. It is allegedly attributed to rote memorisation, the most used practice in traditional classrooms in Pakistan. In the Blooms' taxonomy, the last three stages (analysis, synthesis and evaluation) are considered higher-order skills. These skills are usually assessed with questions of how and why, demanding logic and rationale to answer the questions related to higher-order skills. Most of the students ignore such questions and leave them unattended in the answer sheets. In the Pakistani context, the age of secondary school students is approximately between 13-16 years which is the logical reasoning stage (12 years to onward as cited by Piaget in his age stage model). At this stage, CT skills should be promoted among students, since literature (Ramos, Dolipas, & Villamor, 2013) suggests that CT skills can be developed effectively through different pedagogical practices incorporated by teachers.

The above literature describes different pedagogical practices for the development of CT skills in science students. Therefore, it was of great significance to conduct a study to develop an understanding of how secondary school science teachers interpret Pakistani education policy's recommendations for developing critical thinking skills and how they incorporate them in their classroom practices in public secondary schools.

Statement of the Problem

Critical thinking has become an emerging and significant construct in the teaching-learning process for the twenty-first-century learners and international and national literature emphasise CT skills development among secondary level science students. Due to focus in the Pakistani education policy documents, there are suggested different pedagogical practices for this purpose and rote memorisation emerges as a big hindrance in achieving this aim. The teaching-learning process may be developed through the production of critical thinking students. Therefore, the current study was conducted to compare education policy documents and science teacher practices for developing critical thinking skills among secondary level students.

Aim of the Study

The current study aimed to develop an understanding of how science teachers interpret and enact education policy recommendations for developing critical thinking skills among secondary school students in public schools.

Objectives of the Study

The present study is guided by the following objectives:

(1) To identify education policy documents' recommendations for the development of CT skills among secondary school students.

(2) To explore secondary science teachers' interpretations of education policy documents' recommendations for the development of CT skills among secondary school students in public schools.

(3) To explore secondary science teachers' enactment of education policy documents' recommendations for the development of CT skills among secondary school students in public schools.

(4) To identify gaps between education policy documents' recommendations and science teachers' enactment of recommendations for the development of CT skills among secondary school students in public schools.

Research Questions

This study is guided by the following research questions:

(1) What are the recommendations of education policy documents for the development of CT skills among secondary school students in public schools?

(2) What are the science teachers' interpretations of education policy documents' recommendations for the development of CT skills among secondary school students in public schools?

(3) What are the science teachers' enactment practices related to education policy
documents' recommendations for the development of CT skills among
secondary school students in public schools?

(4) What are the gaps between the education policy documents' recommendations
and science teachers' enactment practices related to the development of CT
skills among secondary school students in public schools?

Significance of the Study

It is asserted that the main aim of science education is to produce critical
thinkers in the contemporary twenty-first century. The international and national
literature and education policy documents have been focusing on CT skills
development in secondary level science students and rote memorisation is being
discouraged because it hinders the process of developing rational thinkers.

The current study will be a fruitful addition to new knowledge and a valuable
contribution towards theory development. The study in hand will be beneficial for
different stakeholders like teachers, students, administrators, educationists, subject
experts, policymakers, curriculum developers, teacher training institutions, future
researchers and ultimately for the society. The gaps will be identified from education
policy documents' analysis and science teachers' practices regarding pedagogy. In the
national and international context, this will be an addition in knowledge and
understanding through policy and practice, which will ultimately contribute to the
existing literature and theoretical expansion.

Primarily, the study will be beneficial for teachers and students and ultimately
for educationists and administrators. The findings of the study will help the
participant teachers in developing a nuanced understanding of the concept of CT and
its importance for science education during the reflection processes involved in the

interviewing processes. They will be aware of such pedagogical practices which may be necessary for CT skills development in science students. In the same way, they may also adopt the assessment system accordingly through how and what type of questions can benefit the achievement of CT skills development. As a result, students will be taught through different relevant pedagogical practices for CT skills development, which will be ultimately beneficial for the students. The Punjab Education Department is focusing on 100 percent retention and zero drop out at the secondary level. Through the learner-centred pedagogical practices, which are used with students' engagement, it will help in student retention and stop drop out.

It will be significant for the policy-makers, curriculum developers and subject experts to revisit and design the documents in the future. With the results of the analysis from education policy documents and science teachers' practices, it might be helpful for policy-makers and curriculum developers to get an understanding of the gap between policy and practices. It might guide them to re-design the policy documents according to perceptions and understanding of the secondary level science teachers for CT skills development. They might update the sections on aims, pedagogical practices and assessment system of the documents accordingly. Subject experts will also gain knowledge and understanding of pedagogical practices for CT skills development in the local Pakistani context.

The findings and recommendations of the current study will be beneficial for the teacher training/professional development and teacher education institutions like Quaid-e-Azam Academy for Educational Development (QAED), Institute of Education and Research (IER), Allama Iqbal Open University (AIOU), University of Education (UE) and other institutions for teacher education and professional development. The findings and recommendations of the study will be helpful for these institutions with regards to the development of CT skills among science students at the secondary level. These institutions may use the knowledge produced in this study to guide and implement those pedagogical practices in BEd, MEd, their pre-service, induction and in-service teachers' professional development training programmes so the ultimate goal of CT skills development in science education may be fulfilled.

The study will be beneficial for the overall society since the main aim of the current study is to analyse education policy documents and science teachers' practices in the development of CT skills among science students to produce a skilled generation for the twenty-first century. Reflective thinking and problem-solving skills are necessary to face the challenges of life in a real situation. Ultimately, CT skills development among the students will guide them towards the progress and development of an individual as well as for the whole society.

Conceptual Framework of the Study

The main aim of the study was to analyse education policy documents and science teachers' practices for developing CT skills at the secondary level. The science teachers' perceptions were found through a self-developed guide for semi-structured interviews and then their practices were explored through classroom observations. Therefore, an action-based belief and practice framework for analysing teaching was used.

There are multiple views regarding the pedagogy of the teachers, but the most commonly used are teacher-centred and learner-centred methods. The action-based framework developed by Alexander (2001) was used for analysing teaching in the current study. This framework consists of three concepts, that is, frame, form and act. The following figure explains the action-based framework for analysing teaching:

Frame	Form	Act
Space		Task
Student Organization	Lesson	Activity
Time		Interaction
Curriculum		Judgment
Routine, Rules and rituals		

Figure 1. 1. An Action-based framework for analysing teaching

Some Key Terms

Science Teachers

In this study, the term 'science teachers' refers to the teachers who are teaching Physics, Chemistry or Biology subjects to 9th and 10th classes in public secondary schools in Punjab.

Critical Thinking Skills

Critical thinking skills in this study refers to the demonstration of skills related to higher-order reasoning. The hierarchical classification of learning behaviours, as proposed by Bloom (1956) was used to interpret these skills. As a result, the last three stages of Bloom's taxonomy: analysis, synthesis and evaluation, considered as higher-order or critical thinking skills were identified.

Pedagogy

Pedagogy is the art and science of teaching. It entails teaching methods and professional practices for teaching in the classroom. These different teaching methods are used by the science teachers in the classrooms.

Education Policy Documents

Education policy documents in this study refer to four education policy documents, which include National Education Policy (NEP, 2009), National Curriculum for Physics, Grades, IX-X (NCP, 2006), National Curriculum for

Chemistry, Grades, IX-X (NCC, 2006) and National Curriculum for Biology, Grades, IX-X (NCB, 2006).

Practices

The actions introduced by teachers in response to the education policy recommendations.

Delimitations of the Study

The current study aimed to develop an understanding of education policy documents and science teachers' practices for developing CT skills at the secondary school level. Therefore, the scope of the study was to analyse education policy documents, that is, National Education Policy (NEP, 2009), National Curriculum for Physics, Chemistry and Biology (2006) regarding the recommendations for the development of CT skills at the secondary level since the focus of the study was based on these documents regarding only grades IX-X. These documents were analysed in the context of different pedagogical practices suggested by policy documents and to be used by science teachers to develop CT skills among secondary school students.

This qualitative research had a multiple case study research design. Through this methodology, an understanding was developed about the participants' multiple viewpoints regarding pedagogical practices for developing CT skills. The multiple cases strengthen the results through replicating the patterns as these provide external validation for the findings (Yin, 2013).

The sample for the current study was obtained through a purposive sampling technique. This type of sampling is used to recruit information-rich participants and to seek in-depth understating of a phenomenon. In qualitative study, sample size is determined by the research purpose and the target population should consist of relevant individuals according to the research purpose (Patton, 2002; Zikmund, Babin,

Carr, & Griffin, 2013). For the sampling of education policy documents, four

education policy documents identified earlier were targeted to analyse pedagogical

practices suggested for the development of CT skills. Twelve science teachers were

selected as research participants through a purposive sampling technique (Patton,

2015). All teachers were selected to ensure comprehensive sample teaching science

subjects, that is, Physics, Chemistry and Biology from four different public secondary

schools fulfilling the purpose of the study. The criteria for the selection was: Teachers

who were teaching Physics, Chemistry or Biology subjects in the selected schools

from the selected geographical area (Faisalabad District, Punjab) and had at least a

minimum of 1 year of teaching experience.

The Structure of the Dissertation

The current dissertation comprises five chapters.

Chapter 1 includes introduction, the background of the study, statement of the

problem, purpose, objectives, research questions, significance, delimitations of the

study, some key terms and the structure of the dissertation.

Chapter 2 discusses the review of the related literature. More specifically, it

discusses the concept of critical thinking, its history and different perspectives, critical

thinking skills, its importance in science education and teaching. Furthermore,

different pedagogical practices and previous empirical studies in the area of the

development of CT skills in the national and international context are discussed.

Chapter 3 is about research methodology. It discusses the purpose of research,

research questions, research design, research sites, sampling, data collection methods,

data analysis and adopted ethical consideration in the dissertation.

Chapter 4 consists of three sections: analysis of education policy documents, semi-structured interviews and classroom observations. All data analysis is discussed in each section.

Chapter 5 consists of findings (policy analysis, teachers' perceptions, practices and classroom observations), discussions and recommendations based on findings.

References and appendices are included at the end of the dissertation.

CHAPTER 2

Review of the Related Literature

Introduction of the Chapter

The current chapter describes nature and a brief history of critical thinking, along with its importance in science education. It also provides the conceptual framework of the study and a review of previous studies related to pedagogical practices for the development of CT in the national and international contexts.

What is Thinking?

Thinking is a mental activity which relies on experience and leads toward new insights. It may be described as a cognitive process of an individual with higher-level skills (Bialik & Fadel, 2015). It consists of different mental operations and thinking skills, which requires capacities and abilities. In the view of Fisher (2011), the process of memory, perceptions, concept formation and language and symbols are the basic cognitive skills for essential learning and problem-solving. In an educational context, thinking may be called an understanding since it is described as 'meaningful learning' (Ausubel, 1978). This meaningful learning has been claimed as opposite of 'rote learning'. In meaningful learning, the new knowledge is linked with the acquired previous knowledge (Khan, 2017).

In literature, thinking is categorized differently. For example, Jerwan (2009) categorized thinking as scientific, analytical, lateral, verbal, reflective, concrete, creative, vertical, inductive, deductive, abstract, mathematical, effective, productive, logical, metacognitive, absolute and philosophical thinking. In addition, Al-Osaimi, Reid, and Rodrigues (2014) shares four categories of thinking, that is, critical, scientific, creative and systematic thinking. Critical thinking is about information questions and its responses with what, how and why. The second type is scientific thinking, about the nature, place and handling of experiments. The third one is creative thinking, which is about the creation and novelty of something. The fourth category is systematic thinking, which is about the understanding of systems for investigation. On the other hand, Khan (2017) professes that thinking is a coherent and integrated process; therefore, the division of thinking into categories is artificial.

What is Critical Thinking?

It is the process of thinking which involves analytical evaluation of a situation, cognitive activity, having mental process including analysis and evaluation. In the theoretical literature, CT is defined differently. Halpern (1997) opines that "Thinking is purposeful, reasoned and goal directed" (p 4), "An active, persistent and careful consideration of a belief or supposed form of knowledge in the light of grounds which support it and further conclusions to which it ends" (Dewey, 2004, p. 6), critical thinking that "Facilitates judgment because it relies on criteria that is self-correcting and sensitive to context" (Lopman, Reacher, Vipond, Sarangi, & Brown, 2004, p. 212). "The art of thinking about your thinking in order to improve your thinking" (Paul & Elder, 2006c, p. xvii), is a purposeful, judgmental and self-regulatory thinking (Facione, 2007) process of decision making based on evidence with logical reasoning for problem-solving (Nugent & Vitale, 2008). Critical thinking comprises logical reasoning and decision of the facts after examining and taking opinions (Fahim & Pezeshki, 2012). This metacognitive process uses analysis, synthesis and inferences, based on domain specific and general knowledge for logical conclusions and solution of different life problems (Garner et al., 2016). Critical thinking is considered reasonable reflecting thinking focused on deciding what to believe or do (Ennis, 2018). Moreover, according to the findings of the Delphi report by American

Philosophical Foundation, a panel of 46 experts described CT as "Purposeful, self-regulatory judgment, which results in interpretation, analysis, evaluation, and inference, as well as explanation of the evidential, conceptual, methodological, criteriological, or contextual considerations upon which that judgment is based." (Facione, 1990, p. 3) In addition, in Bloom's taxonomy, analysis, synthesis and evaluation are called higher order thinking and CT skills (Zhao et al., 2016). Indeed, no singular definition has been used in the literature.

When definitions are compared, CT involves five skills such as analysis, communication, creativity, open mind-ness and problem-solving emerge. First, analysis is the ability for the careful examination regarding a problem, data or text. The individuals having the ability of analysis may examine the prior information. These may include judgment, asking questions, and interpretation. Second, communication is about the sharing of ideas that can find solutions effectively. There are different skills like collaboration, explanation, teamwork, presentation, active listening, assessment, verbal and written communication. Third, creativity is about information patterns to solve them critically. The aspects involved in it are curiosity, flexibility, imagination, inferring, conceptualisation, vision, predicting and synthesising. Fourth, open mindedness is the ability to view without assumptions and judgments with the received information. Ideas should be evaluated without any bias. This includes fairness, humility, diversity, fairness, observation and reflection. Fifth, problem-solving is the skill involved through analysis of a problem with the generation of its hypothesis, implementation and solution with assessment and success of the plan. These skills are innovation, evaluation, decision-making and identifying patterns. Furthermore, different CT skills are also discussed in the literature like inductive and deductive reasoning, integration, brainstorming, project management, SWOT (Strengths, weaknesses, opportunities, threats) analysis, risk management, qualitative and quantitative data management.

Critical Thinking in Different Perspectives

Three primary academic disciplines of philosophy, psychology and education provide roots for the literature on critical thinking (Lai, 2011; Lewis & Smith, 1993). These separate academic disciplines have different concerns with respect to critical thinking; therefore, these different approaches define critical thinking in their respective theoretical literature. Each of these approaches is explored below:

Philosophical perspective of critical thinking places emphasis on a hypothetical critical thinker, describing qualities of the individuals, rather than their behaviours. The eminent proponents of this approach are Socrates, Plato, Aristotle and the most recently include Lipman and Paul (Lai, 2011). It has been described as an ideal type by Sternberg (1986) since it has a focus on the capability of the people to do their best under various circumstances. In the same way, Paul (1995) discusses this in the context of 'perfection of thought'. This approach narrates the critical thinker as mature, flexible, open-minded and well informed; one who understands different points of view and is willing to suspend judgment to take another perspectives (Facione, 1990).

Furthermore, from a philosophical perspective, the emphasis is given on thought strands since Bailin (2002) describes CT as thinking for a specific quality like good thinking which meets a particular criterion. Another focus is on the application of formal rules or logic (Lewis & Smith, 1993; Sternberg, 1986). In this context, CT has been defined by several researchers as reflective and reasonable thinking, skilful and responsible thinking for good, purposeful and self-regulatory judgment with analysis, interpretation and evaluation (Facione, 1990), "The art of analysing and evaluating thinking" (Paul & Elder, 2006c, p. 88), disciplined and self-directed thinking in a reflective way (Facione, 2007). Qualities and standards of thoughts are emphasized in a philosophical perspective as critical thinking is thinking of a specific quality in which good thinking is accurate (Bailin, 2002). Furthermore, this approach focuses on the application of formal rules regarding logic. Despite focusing on logic and rationale, this approach has a limitation of no correspondence to reality (Sternberg, 1986).

In the psychological perspective, CT has been contrasted with the philosophical approach in two aspects. This approach deals with behaviours having more focus on people thinking in ideal circumstances. In this approach, CT has been described as a mental process with decision making and problem-solving strategies (Sternberg, 1986). In the same way, Halpern (2007) is of the view that these cognitive strategies are used to get possible desired outcomes, which considers evidence after seeing both sides when solving problems. CT has been described from the learning point of view. It is a complex mental process consisting of skills and attitudes for decision making and problem-solving skills to achieve desired outcomes, openness and adaptability of mind (Willingham, 2009), identifying arguments, opposing arguments with evidence, identifying unfair assumptions, conclusion with justification and presenting structured point of view with logic (Cottrell, 2011). This approach emphasises cognitive skills which are necessary for CT depending upon the observed behaviours.

Sternberg (1986) has described the educational approach of CT as an ideal type, focusing on the capability of people for their deeds under the best circumstances. In the educational context as described earlier, Bloom's taxonomy is presented in its cognitive domain with its last three levels, which are related to CT skills. For educational practitioners, it has been used in teaching and developing higher-order thinking skills. This cognitive domain of Bloom's taxonomy consists of six levels starting from knowledge to evaluation. The levels included in lower-order thinking are knowledge, comprehension and application. The three highest levels, which include analysis, synthesis and evaluation fall under higher order thinking (Kennedy, Fisher, & Ennis, 1991). The educational approach of CT is based on classroom experiences of many years, which is beneficial in the educational field. It can be used for the promotion of CT skills in the students through three levels of higher-order thinking. The students and teachers focusing on developing these aspects with teaching and assessment methods may get fruitful results regarding CT skills development of the students. According to Sternberg (1986), the educational importance has an advantage by having classroom observations and assessment context.

Two types of modern approaches have been described for the development of CT among students, that is, the approach of curriculum factors and pedagogical factors. Both of these factors have their significant contribution in developing CT skills in the students since both are recommended to be implemented by the teachers (Abrami et al., 2008). For curriculum factors, the infusion approach is used. The immersion method is also used through training, problem-solving skills, teaching conceptual knowledge and collaborative learning. Curriculum factors have a positive relationship with CT skills development (Abrami et al., 2008).

The pedagogical factors are also used to develop CT skills among students like problem-solving, group learning, interactive sessions and case studies. Furthermore, three categories have been designed in pedagogical approaches like active learning, scaffolding and meta-cognition. Active learning has several pedagogical approaches like collaborative learning, experiential learning and problem-based learning. Scaffolding and meta-cognition have also been used for CT skills development.

History of Critical Thinking

CT is an old term. It was used before schools were established (Facione, 2007). It has its roots from Socrates who used it 2500 years ago as reflective thinking since it was the main tool of philosophers for finding the truth through reasoning (Paul & Elder, 2006b) and was being used as 'Socratic questioning'. According to Socrates, individuals should have power and deep insight. He described the importance of asking questions with probing, which leads to different ideas and beliefs (Paul, Elder, & Bartell, 1997). Being a founder of CT paradigm, he focused on reflective questions with common beliefs and explanations to distinguish between reasonable and logical evidence rather than lack of evidence. Evidence was formed through analysing, examining and assuming basic concepts to trace out the implications.

In the 18th century, the concept of CT was extended to develop a power of critical thoughts. In the view of Paul and Elder (2006b), philosophers like Voltaire, Newman, Mill and Sumner continued the Socratic tradition in the 18th and 19th century. The idea of Socratic questioning was developed and used by other different scholars in several fields like Sociology, Language, Economics and Biology (Paul & Elder, 2006b). According to Al-Qasmi (2006), Dewey also used this concept after Socrates with the concept of 'learning by doing'. Ennis (1993) cited the work of Dewey (1910) from his book "How we think" in modern critical thinking. Earlier, this term was used by Glaser (1941) in his work "An Experiment in the Development of Critical Thinking" based on Dewey's work.

In the 20th century, thinking about CT made progress through the power and nature of CT with the explicit formulation. Piaget included egocentric and socio-centric types in human thinking for the development of human thought. Different scholars defined CT with their point of view as Norris and Ennis (1989) with 'reasonable and reflective thinking', focusing on what to do or believe in. In the view of Paul and Elder (2006b), Glaser is the originator of modern critical thinking movement as he praised the Watson-Glaser Critical Thinking Appraisal (Watson, 1980). The concept of 'critical thinking' has been performing a significant role in the current educational scenario.

Later on, Al-Degether (2009) acknowledged the work of Bloom (1956), a cognitive psychologist at Chicago University who used the concept of CT earlier as higher-order thinking. A taxonomy of cognitive skills was developed by the colleagues of Bloom, which was related to critical thinking. Similarly, Al-Qasmi (2006) has described Bloom's (1956) modern critical thinking theory. In the same way, Kong (2001) argues that modern CT was originated in 1962 with the reference of Ennis, focusing on the process of CT with its quality products. This concept was further defined in the late 1980s, as the process of critical thinking for deciding beliefs and actions (Norris & Ennis, 1989).

In the modern history of CT, there are several studies for this concept since 1910 to the present. Accordingly, this concept was initiated in 1910 when Dewey (2004) questioned CT in the early twentieth century with the term 'critical thinking' and reflective thinking in his book "How we think". In the view of Paul and Elder (2006b), 'three waves of critical thinking', particularly in education, are found in the evidence of its history from 1970-1997.

The first wave of critical thinking continued from 1970-1982. This wave was based on reasoning and logic, which was dominated by the philosophers. Its focus was on logic, argumentation and reasoning. In this period, the philosophers started working on CT for education as informal logic and was included as an individual course of CT (Paul et al., 1997). There were two problems in this wave: theoretical problems and pedagogical problem. In the theoretical problem, CT was transferred from informal logic courses to the broader curriculum. On the other hand, the pedagogical problem was about the ambiguity for the students in the application of critical thinking in schools and future.

The second wave was in action from 1980-1993. During this wave, the concept was developed with different perspectives such as critical pedagogy and feminism as critical thinking in various disciplines such as cognitive psychology, business, nursing and biology. In the view of Paul et al. (1997), this wave also has two problems: lack of philosophical foundation in its reformers' theory and the challenge of incorporating critical thinking into instruction across the curriculum (Paul et al., 1997).

The third and the last wave of critical thinking lasted from 1990-1997 and represents a commitment amongst theorists to transcend the main weaknesses of the first two waves and was concerned with integrating 'a comprehensive theory of critical thinking', 'an integrated set of dispositions' and 'a comprehensive concept of logic' (Paul et al., 1997).

The modern critical thinking has been declared as the purpose of education (Halpern, 2014) since Dewey called the CT as 'learning to think'. Furthermore, the inquiry and investigation-based strategies were thought to be useful in the classrooms, rather than just telling them about CT. Accordingly, this was aimed to make the students learn thinking by themselves. Based on that, a scientific-based method model was proposed.

Critical Thinking and Delphi Study

A national Delphi study project was established by the American Philosophical Association in 1988, including Facione and other 46 experts. They came from different disciplines like social sciences, philosophy, education and physical sciences and were involved in a project. They formulated critical thinking and its disposition. The main aim of this study was to explore the notion of CT, identify its effective processes as well as its evaluation. Furthermore, this study aimed to design an educational program for critical thinking as well as its integration in the curriculum. Experts of the study reported the concept of critical thinking and after getting feedback from the experts, Facione (1990) further developed the concept and the process for two years. At the end, experts were able to define critical thinking and its disposition. Cognitive skills were listed as description, elucidation, analysis, assessment, conclusion and self-regulation (Facione, 1990).

The Delphi report gave a comprehensive list of qualities of the ideal critical thinker; they are : well informed, inquisitiveness, open-minded, flexible, trustfulness of reason, fair-minded in evaluation, decision making, willing to review, seek clarity of problems, honesty in facing individual prejudices, reasonability of criteria selection, inquiry focused, orderliness in complicated matters and preserving in result findings (Facione, 1990).

Critical Thinking Skills

The skills that can be used for critical thinking are tools of inquiry, categorisation, analysis, synthesis and evaluation. Different researchers have provided lists for CT skills. According to Martin and Ronald (2015), it includes asking and answering questions, open-mindedness, basis for decision-making, clarification and inference to suppose and integrate the CT abilities. In the view of Facione (2007), these are analysis, interpretation, inference, explanation, self-regulation, evaluation, interpretation and explaining and seeing both sides of an issue. These skills can be developed through thinking about and identifying assumptions (Paul & Elder, 2006b). According to Watson (1980), CT skills are described as recognition of assumptions, interpretations, inferences, deduction and evaluation of argumentation.

Udall and Daniels (1991) classified CT skills into three categories: inductive, deductive and evaluative thinking skills. Inductive thinking is about the inferential process to conclude the available proof. Naturally, this type of thinking works from specific to general as it is regarding the discovery of rules, which is an important way of solving a new problem and its solution for the development of a new hypothesis. Therefore, there is need to make inferences and conclusions for the generalisation to avoid falling into errors (Udall & Daniels, 1991). On the other hand, deductive reasoning is about reasoning from general to specific or top-down approach. It is about the process of logical inference to reach a particular conclusion through the assumption of available knowledge. From this, an inference can be seen necessary through logical deduction in a situation. Evaluative thinking is about the mental activity to issue a judgement regarding the value of thoughts as well as their soundness and ability of judgment for decision making to choose the best option (Udall & Daniels, 1991).

According to Ennis (1991), CT has two features: reasonability due to conductive deduction and sound justification of the decisions and its proof of reflective thinking with complete awareness regarding the steps of thinking of deduction. Three sets of CT skills have been described, which are skills of accurate identification and clarification of the problem, skills related to inference of information and problem-solving skills (Ennis, 1993). According to Jerwan (2009), these groups have been extended as differences between facts, which may be verified or claimed for judgmental statements, judgment about subject related claims and facts, credibility of information source, checking of any biasness, identification of inconstancy of reasoning, decision about the subject and building of solid groundwork.

Facione (1990) has categorised CT skills (inference, interpretation, explanation, analysis and self-regulation) in the following way. The inference has three subcategories: querying evidence, conjecturing alternatives and drawing the conclusion. It has been defined as follows:

> To identify and secure elements needed to draw reasonable conclusions; to form conjectures and hypotheses; to consider relevant information and to reduce the consequences flowing from data, statements, principles, evidence, judgment, beliefs, opinion, concepts, descriptions, questions or other forms of representation" (Facione, 1990, p. 9).

Facione (1990) defines 'interpretation' as "To comprehend and express the meaning or significance of a wide variety of experiences, situations, data, events, judgments, conventions, beliefs, procedures, or criteria." (p. 6). It has been divided into three sub-skills: categorisation, decoding sentences and clarifying meanings.

'Explanation' has been defined by Facione (1990) as "To state and to justify that reasoning in terms of the evidential, conceptual, methodological, criteriological and contextual considerations upon which one's results were based; and to present one's reasoning in the form of cogent arguments" (p. 10). It has three subcategories: with starting results, justifying procedures and presenting arguments.

Facione (1990) defines 'analysis' as "To identify the intended and actual inferential relationships among statements, questions, concepts, descriptions of other forms of representation, intended to express belief, judgment, experiences, reasons, information or opinions" (p. 7). It has different subcategories as examining ideas, identifying and analysing arguments. The evaluation has two subcategories, having the following definition:

> To assess the credibility of statement or other representations which are accounts or descriptions of a person's perception, experience, situation, judgment, belief or opinion; and to assess the logical strength of the actual or intended inferential relationships among statements, description, questions or other forms of representation (Facione, 1990, p. 8).

Facione (1990) defines 'self-regulation' as "Self-consciously to monitor one's cognitive activities, the elements used in those activities, and the results educed, particularly by applying skills in analysis and evaluation to one's inferential judgments with a view toward questioning, confirming, validating, or correcting either one's reasoning or one's results" (p. 10). It has two subcategories, that is, self-examination and self-correction.

According to Facione (1990), as the result of the Delphi report stated that an individual must have core skills of critical thinking. Various authors have claimed critical thinking to be a vital goal of education (Kong, 2001; Norris & Ennis, 1989). Moreover, some argue different common principles of critical thinking (Ennis, 2001; Fisher, 2011; Halpern, 1997) with different CT skills. These traits identify the elements of reasoning and conclusion, identification and evaluation of assumptions, clarification and interpretation of expression and ideas, the judgment of acceptance, credibility regarding claims, evaluation of different types of arguments, to draw the inference and analysis and evaluation to draw inferences and production of arguments. Clarke (1993) is of view that CT is not about the list of skills rather the capacity to use these skills for making a successful plan. A learner may use only critical thinking after willingness to accept them as this type of thinking is useful and appropriate (Alosaimi, 2013).

Critical Thinking and other kinds of Thinking

In literature, different types of thinking have been described. These types are explained as follows:

Scientific Thinking

Scientific thinking concerns thinking about the content regarding science and the reasoning process. It has been described as the involvement of the skills to generate a test and revise the theories and then reflect on the process of acquiring knowledge (Kuhn & Franklin, 2006; Wilkening & Sodian, 2005). Al-Ahmadi and Mahmood (2008) explains scientific thinking as "The application of the methods or principles of scientific thinking inquiry to reasoning or problem-solving situations" (p. 108). In the view of Willingham (2019), scientific thinking is associated with critical thinking and requires domains specific knowledge regarding science subjects. Both scientific and critical thinking have different characteristics. Rationale and scepticism are the basics of scientific thinking as well as empiricism associated with science. Furthermore, both scientific and critical thinking are viewed similarly when scientists practise critical thinking.

Creative Thinking

Creative thinking is the application of imagination to find out a solution (Paul & Elder, 2006b). These skills are different from CT skills with open, relax and playful resources and at the same time involve risk-taking. These skills look forward to many answers to a question, to make crazy suggestions and judgment of ideas (Cottrell, 2011). Creativity has been described as having a relationship with critical thinking by several researchers (Paul & Elder, 2006b) and both of these constructs seem mutually exclusive at first glance. According to Bailin (2002), there is a need for creativity for critical thinking. In the same way, Paul and Elder (2006b) are of the view that both concepts are aspects of good purposeful thinking. These should be integrated during instruction for positive outcomes. The idea of creative thinking has also been used widely in literature, art, science and technology development with different styles and designs.

There are similarities and differences between critical and creative thinking. Both types of thinking are interconnected with each other since problem-solving and evaluation of the arguments are required in both. Some researchers claim a similarity between CT and creative thinking, while others make a clear distinction between both concepts. For example, in the view of Paul (1995), due to purposeful thinking and the ability of individuals to work things out, both terms are similar. In the same way, Ennis (2018) and Halpern (2007) are also of the same stance that critical thinking demands several cognitive skills to develop hypothesis, problem solving by using creative thinking. Creativity and CT are considered advanced ways of thinking (Damas, 2007) and evaluation of arguments is required in both types (Glassner & Schwarz, 2007).

Hartman and Sternberg (1992) describe the contrast regarding the functions of critical and creative thinking. Critical thinking makes an individual capable of decision making, while creative thinking develops, combines and changes ideas and information into a new reality. Furthermore, these may be different in terms of their aims. According to this description, creative thinking aims to develop new ideas, while critical thinking aims in evaluating and assessing plans. Nonetheless, both types are useful in deductive and scientific reasoning.

Reflective Thinking

Reflective thinking is also an essential type of thinking which could be interchangeable for critical thinking. It has been narrated as 'reflective thinking' by Dewey (1933), in his book "How we think". Furthermore, he has described it as "Active, persistent, and careful consideration of any belief or supposed form of knowledge in the light of the grounds which support it" (p. 6). It can be understood that self-reflection which is also a skill is used for the improvement of thinking; therefore, reflection plays a significant role in the development of CT skills since it has been described as thinking about thinking for its improvement (Elder & Paul, 2019). Some of the researchers represent these two types of thinking skills. A few others define it as a form of reflective thinking. For example, Norris and Ennis (1989) has explained the definition as "A reasonable, reflective thinking that is focused on deciding what to believe or do" (p.4). In the view of Phan (2008), reflective thinking is a tool to improve learning as meaningful, which also helps the students in developing CT skills. Furthermore, he describes reflective thinking as metacognitive skill which is described as follows.

In the previous cited literature, there is an ongoing debate regarding metacognition (Moseley et al., 2005). Metacognition is described as thinking about thinking, knowledge about thinking and learning activities. It is also about awareness of own thinking, content, monitoring of cognitive process and thoughts (Martinez, 2006). Metacognition is involved in the components of critical thinking (Pithers & Soden, 2000; Swartz, 2003; Tsai, 2001). According to Kuhn and Franklin (2006), the process or outcome can be addressed as it serves as a bridge between education and critical thinking.

Metacognition has a role in supporting students' autonomy. Accordingly, teachers must adopt the habit of learning how to question and also monitor them with ownership (Moseley et al., 2005; Swartz, 2003). Similarly, in the view of Ben-David and Orion (2013), metacognition is necessary for science classrooms and self-regulating learning. There is a strong relationship between CT, Bloom's Taxonomy, socio-constructivist approaches and metacognition (Moseley et al., 2005).

Self-regulation and motivation have a connection with CT too and some researchers have narrated the relationship between self-regulation with critical thinking. According to the Delphi report, self-regulation is the skill of critical thinking (Facione, 2007). Different researchers are of the view that critical thinking includes both skills and dispositions. Disposition for critical thinking has been defined as the inner motivation for decision making with critical thinking (Facione, 2007). Therefore, motivation is seen as an important requirement of critical thinking skills and abilities. According to some motivational researchers, challenging tasks of higher-order thinking skills are a source of motivation more than rote memorisation (Turner, 1995).

Bloom's Taxonomy and Critical Thinking

Bloom's taxonomy was presented in 1956 by Bloom and his companions with its three domains of learning, that is, cognitive, affective and psychomotor. The cognitive domain is directed towards the thinking process with six different levels. These levels include knowledge, comprehension and application, which are referred to lower-order thinking skills (LOTS), and the last three levels are analysis, synthesis, and evaluation which are known as higher-order thinking skills (HOTS). These levels are in an arranged hierarchy from easy to difficult for the development of CT.

In Bloom's Taxonomy, some terms are confusing when applying Bloom's Taxonomy (Krathwohl, 2002). Thus, Bloom's Taxonomy was revised. In this taxonomy, there are different categories with a brief description and definition regarding that particular cognitive process of thinking. With revised Bloom's taxonomy, the stages are remembering (knowledge), applying (application), analysing (analysis), evaluating (evaluation) and creation (synthesis).

Teachers can use this taxonomy for the development of students' learning outcomes and CT skills. Bloom's Taxonomy has been helpful in discussions of critical thinking (Ennis, 1993; Facione, 1990; Halpern, 2007). Teachers may engage the students according to different levels of questions. These levels are described as below:

Knowledge

In Bloom's Taxonomy, the first level is knowledge, which is about recalling the information. In this level, remembrance is required as it was learnt. In this level, just definitions, facts and observations of the past are learnt. Questions starting with what and who are part of this level, like what is the definition of air? Or who was the first governor-general of Pakistan? For the formulation of objectives at this level, different verbs are used like define, recall, who, list, identify, recognise, name, remember, etc.

Comprehension

The second level requires an understanding of the information from the students. In order to answer comprehension questions, students must go through remembering or recalling the information. For example, what do you think Iqbal means when he asks this quote? Usually, such questions require students to interpret or translate the material presented: What is the main idea of the chart presented here?

The information regarding comprehension should be provided to the students earlier. The different verbs used for this type of questions are, describe, compare, contrast, etc.

Application

After memorisation and understanding, the students must apply the information in a specific situation. Questions at this level are based on the application of using information from previous knowledge and understanding to solve a specific problem or question, for example, in Maths within different formulas like if $x=2$ and $y=5$, then $x+2y=$? The words used to formulate questions of application are apply, use, classify, choose, employ, show, translate, make, illustrate, demonstrate, record, etc.

Analysis

Analysis type questions are related to higher-order thinking which demands in-depth and critical thinking. Such questions ask reasoning and evidence to respond. These questions identify the reasons, motives and causes within a specific position, like why did he decide to skip the job? These questions do not only help the students about learning what happened, but also find the reasons behind that happening. The words used are why, compare/contrast, summarize, investigate, justify, deduce, etc.

Synthesis

The questions regarding synthesis also belong to higher-order thinking skills which can demand creative thinking. These questions are used to make predictions and solve problems. Synthesis is different from analysis since such type of questions have more than one answer. These questions are of different kinds like production of original communication, for making predictions and to solve problems. The words used to describe are predict, produce, develop, design, write, synthesise, create, invent, estimate, combine, hypothesise, etc.

Evaluation

The last level of Bloom's taxonomy is evaluation and the questions asked have more than one answer. This type requires the learners to judge and to decide on a problem. Opinions on issues are also sought at this level like how you will assess the performance of a teacher in the school? To make a judgment on an issue or idea, there must be some criteria. The words used to ask questions are argue, judge, evaluate, assess, select, verify, recommend, conclude, etc.

Importance of Critical Thinking

CT is considered among twenty-first-century skills because of its importance in developing "Economic, technological, informational, demographic and political forces" (Bialik & Fadel, 2015, p. 4). The educational institutions are ensuring that the learners are equipped to function "In a multitasking, multi-faceted, technology-driven, diverse, vibrant world" (Bialik & Fadel, 2015, p. 4) and the development of CT skills are crucial for this purpose.

To cope with the fast, effective and growing changes in the learners, education should address the issue of students' learning as to how to learn, instead of what to learn, since today's knowledge may provide negligible assistance to solve the dynamic problems of the future. Tsui (2002) is also in favour of teaching students how to learn rather than what to learn. Teachers must teach the students how to think in order to prepare them to tackle different challenges which they may face in their personal, professional life as well as in becoming responsible citizens. Tsui (2002) explains:

> We need to teach them how to think. Higher-order cognitive skills such as the ability to think critically are invaluable to students' futures; they prepare individuals to tackle a multitude of challenges that they are likely to face in their personal lives, careers, and duties as responsible citizens (p. 740).

CT is among the twenty-first-century skills and integral part for the attainment of positive outcomes of students in an educational context. According to Halpern (2007), it is the intellectual skill of how to learn and think about information. Furthermore, in the revolutionary and changing world, CT has become an integral part of the growth and survival of social and economic context (Paul, 1995). Thinking critically has been reflected as essential for positive educational outcomes (Spatariu et al., 2016). Learning CT skills is essential to become an effective reflective thinker (Higgins, 2015).

A framework for twenty-first-century learning was developed in 2007 by the educators and experts of the USA regarding the students' success in life and to become decision maker citizens. This framework (p21, 2007) describes different aspects of twenty-first-century learning skills. In the learning and innovation skills factor, a framework of 4 Cs has been developed including critical thinking, communication, collaboration and creativity. CT has been a buzz word all over the world. It is needed in different phases of life for academic success, employment and professional development. In the view of Hatcher (2006), CT is a necessary skill due to its importance at the workplace, helping in mental in spiritual questioning, evaluating people, policies and institutions as well as to solve social problems. In the beginning, the ability to question and evaluate is the basic level of CT. Attributes needed for CT are analysing information, situation or context, using abstract ideas, open mind ness and effective communication with others.

Importance of CT in Education and Teaching

Critical thinking has a vital importance in the educational setting. Education should be based on reflective thinking regarding the value of education for an individual and the society (Dewey, 2004). It is an essential phenomenon for the progress and development of an individual, for the education system and a self-corrective human notion with profound thinking. It promotes CT skills with dispositions which are the foundation of a logical, sensible, and democratic society (Facione, 1990) where schools and classrooms should deal according to the life context so that their students may represent in real-life learning activities (Gutek, 2013).

CT has its importance because of its role in learner-centred teaching. Dewey focuses on a learner-centred approach, which is supportive of different beliefs of how students learn (Schiro, 2012). In the learner-centred approach, Dewey's social learning theory and educational beliefs can be seen in the context of the classroom as a social entity for students' problem solving like a community. In such classes, students are unique individuals, busy in the constructing their meaning rather than imposing knowledge. Students may learn by doing with problem-solving through hand-on activities (Schiro, 2012). The concept of 'learning by doing' is given by Dewey, whose work and philosophy have been very influential over the years (Theobald, 2009). The philosophy suggests that children must focus on the educational process, as the main aim in education is students' active learning (Schiro, 2012).

Educational process has two principle patterns: standard and reflective (Lopman et al., 2004). According to the standard pattern, education is about the transformation of knowledge, which is considered explicit where teachers are knowledge givers, while students are the receivers of the educational process. On the other hand, the reflective pattern has some principles, that is, education as inquiry, the community of inquiry, reasonable in the context, seek and examine the relationship, thinking in the disciplines and autonomy. In a reflective pattern, the inquiry is about discussion, and questioning the specific subject matter of the discipline. In this context, the CT of students is the real goal (Lopman et al., 2004). Critical thinking is not just a pathway of education, but it is a pathway of the thinking application skills for individuals (Lopman et al., 2004). Teachers as well as students are required to convey and implement these skills.

Teachers play a significant role in promoting CT skills. In the view of Willingham (2019), teachers must ask questions regarding the incorporation of critical thinking. Since the teachers must practise CT for their personal empowerment of CT among themselves; therefore, without realisation and support of the students for the improvement of CT skills development, teachers may play an important role. Similarly, students are encouraged to broaden their learning experiences. Some theorists have considered CT as a natural thinking process as the practice is necessary to improve CT. According to Willingham (2009), teachers can use different teaching strategies to encourage students and make the content more accessible for their better understanding. Four main elements of the learning process have been discussed above that have a great impact on teaching strategies: content, learning material, learners, teachers and organisations.

Importance of Critical Thinking in Science Education

Critical thinking plays a significant role in science education. In the view of Yacoubian (2015), CT is the foundation in science education for fostering scientific knowledge in the future citizens. There are two fundamental roles described in science practice and education. One is linked with the responsibility regarding the use of science and technology in democracy, and the second is the practice related scientific teaching-learning process. Critical questioning along with the ability of question formulation is the most crucial aspect in science education (Demir, 2015;

Osborne, 2014). In addition, science is based on hypotheses, theories, and processes of observations and experiments.

In the Pakistani context, all education policy documents emphasise the development of CT skills in different contexts. In the NEP (2009), the aim of education, curriculum and SLOs have focused on developing CT skills for the twenty-first-century learners. To make the students responsible members of the society, critical and analytical abilities are mentioned as the aim of education. The objectives of education have been described "To develop a self-reliant individual, capable of analytical and original thinking, a responsible member of society and a global citizen" (NEP, 2009, p. 19). Similarly, the curriculum of Physics aims at developing problem-solving and other different skills among secondary school students. The aim of Physics curriculum has been narrated as "To develop the ability to describe and explain concepts, principles, systems, processes and applications related to physics and develop the thinking process, imagination, ability to solve problems, data management, investigating and communication skills" (NCP, 2006, p. 5). The curriculum of Chemistry also aims to produce independent thinkers for solving real situation problems. It is discussed as "An ability to apply the understanding of Chemistry to relevant problems (including those from everyday real-life) and to approach those problems in rationale ways" (NCC, 2006, p. 2). The students must use science and technology for the identification of problems, and bringing creative solutions in their personal, social and professional lives. The document describes as "The aim of the Chemistry curriculum is to produce students who will be capable of doing independent thinking, asking questions, and looking for answers on their own" (NCC, 2006, p. 1). The Biology curriculum also stresses on CT skills development. It can be seen through the description as, "To enable all students to develop their capacities as successful learners, confident individuals, responsible citizens and effective contributors to society" (NCB, 2006, p. 1). In all of these cases, emphasis is given on conceptual and reasoning-based study to find out the solutions in real-life problems. Learning outcomes of all domains of Bloom's Taxonomy are discussed for implementation.

The importance of CT has been discussed in all education policy documents. Different innovative skills are suggested in NEP (2009), with the discouragement of rote learning. In the policy document, it has been explained as "Efforts have to be made to address this issue and need for inculcating critical and analytical thinking skills for producing life-long independent learners have to be emphasised" (NEP, 2009, p. 48). The Physics curriculum focuses on in-depth conceptual understanding through problem-solving. It can be seen in the passage of identified focusing areas as "Emphasis on real-life applications of concepts and problem-solving techniques" (NCP, 2006, p. 3) and "Hence, there is a need to provide the learners with sufficient conceptual background of physics which would eventually make them competent to meet the challenges of academic and pre-professional courses after the secondary level" (NCP, 2006, p. 1).

The Chemistry curriculum underscores that students are expected to show curiosity about the natural world and technology development. They should solve problems through observations, reasoning and investigation. Having scientific and technological knowledge, they should be creative and decision-makers. Aims and objectives of the curriculum present the importance of CT as one of the aims is to develop the abilities in the students to solve the problems of daily life by applying rationale and conceptual understanding. The standards described in the document also focus on CT skills development as they are based on higher-order thinking for conceptual knowledge with the application, analysis and evaluation. The Biology curriculum also focuses on developing CT skills among students. They learn about the interaction of living things through questioning, problem-solving and decision-making strategies. They must be able to identify the problems, conduct and design experiments, and communicate the findings by using different innovative tools.

Furthermore, one point among aims and objectives is to help the students to develop "Capacities to express themselves coherently and logically, both orally and in writing, and to use appropriately modes of communication characteristic of scientific work" (NCB, 2006, p. 8). Student-centred interactive approaches are recommended to be used for the development of CT skills such as, engagement, questioning, problem-solving, discussion, debates, practical work, group work and cooperative learning. It is stressed that the assessment system should also be based on analysis, synthesis, evaluation, problem-solving and analytical thinking. Key focus should be at the assessment of higher abilities of the students. In addition, practical examinations should be conducted to explore problem solving, daily life experiences and investigation skills of the students. Formative assessment is discussed with different techniques like lab completion, worksheets, quizzes, review questions, observations, oral presentations and classroom discussions to achieve the objectives of the curriculum. In the final evaluation strategy, overall 85% weight is suggested to be given for knowledge, comprehension, application, synthesis and evaluation. Furthermore, when assessing theory, 40% of the questions should be designed to measure higher abilities based on problem solving and application of the information. Question papers for the assessment are suggested as curriculum-based rather than a textbook for the evaluation of problem-solving and CT skills.

In international literature too, CT skills have been emphasised in relation to their importance in science education. According to Bailin (2002), CT should be an integral element of science education. Yacoubian (2015) describes different reasons and concludes that CT contributes to the formation of a democratic society with benefits for personal, ethical, cultural and political contexts, and understanding of scientific knowledge.

Importance of CT is increasing gradually in all societies (Demir, 2015) and science subjects are increasingly focusing on critical thinking, since it helps in developing the argumentation and decision-making skills of the students. In short, critical thinking plays a significant role in application and practice of the scientific process in observation and exploration, defining problems, identifying and defining the scientific problem, appropriate solution of the problem, making decisions, critical questioning, question formulation, construction of reliable knowledge, argumentation, discussion and debates, evaluation and rigorous testing and clarification of meanings.

In the view of Bailin (2002), the characteristics of the problem and context where thinking occurs are not a procedure for critical thinking as it needs to be heuristic and helpful in problem-solving. Furthermore, the knowledge of critical thinking must be seen in terms of process (Bailin, 2002). Moreover, he says that the subject knowledge must be sound before the start of CT as it is a necessary part of it. The interpretation consists of bringing out meaning and successful interpretation involving "An understanding of the conventions of representation in the area and the application of the relevant criteria of meaning. These centrally involve knowledge" (Gilbert, 2006, p. 252). Furthermore, he argues that the focus should be on tasks and problem-solving in CT. It also involves the concentration of specific criteria for comprehension and problem-solving. CT is the process of skills and mastering "Other

intellectual resources is insufficient if an individual does not have a basic

commitment to rational inquiry" these are required critical thinking (Bailin, 2002).

Two forms of thinking are described as critical thinking and reflective

thinking. Gilbert (2006) argues that teachers with thinking critically in scientific

perspective have an important place in education. Therefore, teachers training in CT

skills development is crucial for the improvement of future generations.

According to Al-Karaki (2007), critical thinking in science education may be

promoted through different suggestions, that is, diverting of students' attention

towards specific problems regarding information, requirement of activities regarding

issues and problems for the attention and interest to challenge the mind, to raise

doubts about logical interrelation of outcomes, to direct the student for the reflection

of their thinking for suitable solutions, encouragement of students for the engagement

in dialogue and discussion and to express their opinion with evidence. It may be

concluded that good thinking is critical thinking. The deductive approach is mostly

used for science teaching, which is also termed as top-down transmission. In such a

method, the teacher presents different concepts of science and explanation with

logical deduction, and examples for its application. The other approach is based on

the inductive process or a bottom-up approach. These are more observations and

experimentations in which students make inferences of knowledge with the guidance

of their teachers. This approach is related to inquiry-based or problem-based learning.

In the twenty-first century, inquiry-based pedagogy is essential for the interest and

motivation of the students as well as the quality of science education. There is an

excellent need for self-regulation and metacognition for science education (Schraw,

Crippen, & Hartley, 2006). Generally, the process of CT is related to research and

scientific methods like exploration and observation (Demir, 2015) and the construction of reliable knowledge (Osborne, 2014). To achieve these objectives, inquiry-based learning, collaborative support, instruction for critical thinking and problem solving, use of technology and impact of teachers on students' belief is also needed. In literature, practical skills have also been discussed which may be linked with critical thinking and science like the practice of debate, discussion and argumentation (Osborne, 2014), problem-solving (Demir, 2015), evaluation and rigorous testing (Osborne, 2014), assessment, evaluation and rejection of arguments (Brown & Ganguly, 2003), decision making (Vieira, Tenreiro-Vieira, & Martins, 2011) and problem-solving and identification (Demir, 2015).

How to Teach Critical Thinking?

There are three basic schools of thought regarding the teaching of CT skills (Al-Karaki, 2007; Al Heela, 2002; Guttami, 2005). The first school of thought claims that the teaching of CT should occur as a separate subject. The second one is in favour of integrating CT as domain-specific teaching for a specific subject. The last and third school of thought integrates both approaches.

Since CT has been recognized as an essential phenomenon in the educational context, it is necessary to teach CT to the learners of the twenty-first century. In the view of Halpern (1997), different researchers claim that CT skills and abilities can be taught to the students. There are two instructional programs for the improvement of CT skills and abilities. The first one is teaching of problem-solving skills based on Piaget's concept for cognitive development. The second aspect is specific instruction for problem-solving, which has proved to be a positive impact on CT skills development (Kennedy et al., 1991).

There are four instructional approaches for teaching critical thinking, that is, generic, infusion, immersion and mixed (Ennis, 1993). These approaches have been explained as follows.

In the generic approach, explicit course objectives are separated from specific subjects. There is a particular focus on learning critical thinking and dispositions in this approach, with an emphasis on CT skills importance. Furthermore, Socratic questions, Socratic seminar, asking questions, reading notes, discussions of small groups and reflection are included in this approach. Socratic seminar is all about teaching strategies, which may be used for the engagement of critical thinking, listening and communication. It is a forum where students are allowed to discuss and teachers work as facilitators. The main goal is not to answer the questions, rather develop critical thinking.

The infusion approach consists of in-depth subject matter instruction and explicit instruction on general principles of CT. In this approach, critical thinking is encouraged within a specific content area. There is also focus on learning critical thinking and disposition. Importance of CT can also be emphasised in it with the positive impact of this approach. In each class session, there is an emphasis on CT skills development and dispositions. It may be practised through small group discussions, reflections, critical examination of journal articles, fishbowl and think-out-loud activities.

In the immersion approach, methods of CT are not taught explicitly. Instead, these emerge from in-depth examination of a specific subject. For example, students are engaged in deep and thoughtful activities regarding the subject matter and receive feedback on their thinking ability. This encourages their CT skills development. CT skills and abilities are not the focus of direct and explicit instruction, but students may acquire these skills by engagement of subject matter (Ennis, 1991).

The mixed-method approach is the combination of both generic and subject-specific approaches. In both components, explicit instructions for CT can be incorporated (Ennis, 1991). In this approach, students receive subject-specific instructions for CT with a combination of general principles of teaching. In the content area, the emphasis is given on critical thinking. It also increases the understanding of the content with decision making to everyday life. Students learn to apply the skills for argument analysis, open mind-ness and cognitive biases.

Different types of instructions are suggested by Piaget (1936) and Vygotsky (1934), who emphasise social interaction for the promotion of cognitive development. Piaget's age stage model explains the cognitive development, which describes a progression from operational thinking, logical thinking and systematic manipulation of symbols (higher-order thinking skills). Piaget was the first person who conducted studies based on cognitive development, which were based on tests of his children. The stages of Piaget are the sensorimotor, pre-operational, concrete operational and formal operational stage. The sensorimotor stage ranges from birth to 2 years. This stage describes the coordination of senses with motor responses of the children. The pre-operational stage ranges from 2 to 7 years of age. At this stage, children symbolise items and use their imagination during their play. They communicate by speaking about themselves, while they cannot think about the task done by others. This communication is called egocentric. The concrete operational stage is the next stage of Piaget's cognitive development. The age range of this stage is from 7 to 11 years. At the age of 7, children start to think cognitively in a different way and learn to see others' perspective. At this stage of cognitive development, children develop the ability of logical thinking. It is a way to assess and analyse thinking before making any conclusion. During this stage, children learn through using logical thought process with physical objects. Therefore, the connection between this stage and critical thinking can be seen. Now they are about to start the conversational skills. The formal operational stage is the final stage of Piaget's cognitive development. It ranges from 11 years to adulthood. At this stage, adolescents can think abstractly as well as critically. After completion of the concrete operational stage, children begin to control different ideas at a time. It can be done only after thinking creatively using abstract reasoning and explaining outcomes of the problem and also making conclusions. While entering the formal stage, children use problem-solving techniques by learning overtime, which is regarding the development of CT. The secondary level science students of the current study belonged to the same age of formal operational stage who were focused on the development of CT skills.

Vygotsky (1980) consolidated the major concepts of cognitive development by giving the idea of Zone of Proximal Development (ZPD). His argument was to assess the students' ability for problem-solving rather than knowledge acquisition, which results from collaborative learning. Critical thinking is purposeful thinking, which leads to questioning and may be encouraged through social learning. Two approaches have been recognized, which are scaffolding and ZPD. Scaffolding was the idea proposed by Bruner, which refers to an instruction, which results in techniques to move learners and teachers in a progressive way towards strong understanding as well as greater independence in the learning process. Bruner uses this concept as "The steps…taken to reduce the degrees of freedom in carrying out some tasks so that the child can concentrate on the difficult skill that is in the process of acquiring" (As cited in Gibbons, 2013, p. 16).

The scaffolding concept is extended widely into many areas of learning (Turuk, 2008) with an experienced individual providing support for less qualified individuals. It is a natural process through which parents guide and support their kids as it is seen in schools.

Different researchers have suggested specific instructional strategies for the encouragement of CT skills and abilities like questioning, explicit instructions, cooperative learning, collaborative learning, discussion, inquiry-based practices, modelling, active learning, debates and constructivist techniques. Explicit instruction might be used for the development of CT skills (Abrami et al., 2008; Halpern, 1997).

Cooperative learning is a recommended technique for the development of CT skills among students (Abrami et al., 2008; Huang et al., 2017; Nezami, Asgari, & Dinarvand, 2013; Paul & Elder, 2006b; Royhana, Sumiharsono, & Septory, 2021; Ting & Abdullah, 2020). Cooperative learning is a subset of collaborative learning in which students work in groups. It is a method where students often work in pairs or threes to achieve a common goal. In the process, students are actively, within small groups. Social interaction with the usage of dialogue can be seen in scaffolding. In the process of collaborative learning, ideas are exchanged actively, within small groups resulting in the promotion of students' CT. This process involves of discussion; students have responsibility with shared learning.

Furthermore, besides explicit instruction and collaboration, there are several other strategies for the promotion of critical thinking. Student-centred techniques and methods should be used (Paul, 1995). Teachers should model critical thinking during their instruction through reasoning. It may also be practised through 'thinking aloud' as students may observe the teacher using proof and logic to support arguments and assertions (Facione, 2007; Paul, 1995).

Discussion with questioning also has been proved to be significant for the development of CT skills (Bevan, 2017; Khan, 2017). Many scholars indicate, questions have an essential place in the acquisition of CT skills. Students should be asked open-ended, challenging, inquiry, analysis and assessment-based questions. It is called as a thinking driven through questioning and plays a key role in developing critical thinking. There is a need of what, who, where and when type and analytical questions (why and how) for critical thinking development. Questioning techniques have been used by several researchers in their studies (Inamullah, Bibi, & Irshadullah, 2016; Khorraminejad, Ashayeri, Abtahi, Mohammakhani, & Soleimani, 2021; Rashid & Qaisar, 2016; Santos, 2017). In this approach, students can solve their problems and get solutions for real-life situations. For purposeful and productive learning, the questioning technique is effective (Conner, Coppley, & Furr, 2017). In science subjects, inquiry and curiosity are the most critical factors for effective questioning (Ramnarain, 2011). This approach stimulates the students' minds for probing questions to answers in the right way (Paul & Elder, 2006b). In this approach, students can exchange their ideas according to the context, exploring problems and providing a solution for their implication in a real-life situation. Students may be engaged in CT skills through different kinds of questions. After taking answers from the students, teachers must ask how they reached the specific solution for their cognitive development and reasoning ability and get feedback on their responses for their further CT skills development.

Apart from questioning, other different techniques are used for the development of CT skills like inquiry-based practice (Agustini & Suyatna, 2018; Phonna, Safitri, & Syukri, 2021; Sutiani, Situmorang, & Silalahi, 2021), inquiry-based learning (Duran & Dökme, 2016; Sutiani et al., 2021), guided inquiry method

(Azizmalayeri, MirshahJafari, Sharif, Asgari, & Omidi, 2012), active learning (Kim, Sharma, Land, & Furlong, 2013; Rossi et al., 2020), debates (Larsson, 2021; Othman, Sahamid, Zulkefli, Hashim, & Mohamad, 2015; Wahyuni, Qamariah, Syahputra, Yusuf, & Ganin, 2020), discussion, questioning and practical work (Alosaimi, 2013) and problem-based learning (Chen, 2015). These techniques have been studied by different researchers for the development of CT skills among students.

Pedagogy for Critical Thinking

Pedagogy is the art or science of teaching and teaching practice including teaching styles, assessment and feedback. It concerns instructional techniques and strategies of learning, interaction with the teacher and learner for quality education. Siraj-Blatchford, Muttock, Sylva, Gilden, and Bell (2002) define it as:

> The instructional techniques and strategies that allow learning to take place. It refers to the interactive process between teacher/practitioner and learner, and it is also applied to include the provision of some aspects of the learning environment (including the concrete learning environment, and the actions of the family and community" (p. 10).

Critical thinking pedagogy is all about the development of teaching strategies which foster and develop CT among students. According to Grigg (2019), "I advocate both an explicit and infused approach to teaching critical thinking" (p. 1). He further says, "By infusing CT strategies into regular course content-delivery, there is the required, explicit instruction about CT with the added focus on using it in the daily activities of teaching." (p.1). Other pedagogical practices have been discussed in literature which are explained in the next section.

Pedagogical Practices for Developing Critical Thinking Skills

Pedagogy for the development of CT skills has been suggested by global literature as well as national policy documents in the Pakistani context. The activity-based methods are found to be more enjoyable and productive in developing CT skills. In the view of Moon (2008), different methods, techniques and pedagogical practices have been discussed in the literature for the development of CT skills. CT is linked with activities of reflection and arguments in students' learning. It is designed to develop skills like analysis, synthesis and evaluation with decision making. In the literature, student-centred, and activity-based methods have been found more productive for CT skills development with the activities which demand reflection and argumentation with analysis, synthesis and evaluation for decision making. Different methods may influence teaching CT to learners of any subject. The pedagogical practices suggested in the literature for developing CT skills are questioning, problem-solving, inquiry-based methods (Hooks, 2010; Orlich et al., 2012), cooperative/collaborative learning, conversation, group discussion, debate (Fung, 2014). In the four National Education Policy documents: NEP (2009) and National Curriculum for Physics, Chemistry and Biology (2006), the suggested pedagogical practices are questioning, inquiry and problem-solving techniques, cooperative learning, discussion, active involvement, conversation and learning by doing for the development of CT skills among secondary level students.

The following pedagogical practices are considered for the development of CT skills in the literature.

Cooperative Learning

Cooperative learning (CL) has been described by Woolfolk (2004) as a learning system where students work in an ability group and they are encouraged to work together to accomplish a common task. It is an approach of small group learning in which both individual and group are responsible for the overall achievement. It is a method of teaching and learning in which students are formed in different groups for a common task. For many decades, it has been used by researchers working in small teams.

The concept of CL is ancient, but in the educational context, it is considered new as a learning approach, and it has been proved an essential instructional strategy (Johnson & Johnson, 2009). However, the idea of cooperative learning was flourished by Frances Parker in early 19th century.

Igel and Urquhart (2012) propagate three principles for cooperative learning and implementation. First explicit teaching of group process and the interpersonal skills. Students need instructions in the shape of small groups, called interpersonal and group processing skills. The second principle is establishing the goal structure within the groups. In this technique, all members work for a shared goal and are like a unit and team. In this situation, relations are built through interdependence because actions may affect the whole team. The third characteristic is to provide a mechanism for individual accountability. Different ways have been described for individual accountability. As in the view of Johnson and Johnson (2009), groups may include 3 to 5 members. In another way, each group member is expected to learn a specific portion of the lesson and may teach it to the teammates. Social learning experiences have been called as group learning or cooperative learning. Social and constructivists theorists are also of the view that human beings acquire extensive knowledge when interacting with one another.

Different studies provide evidence regarding the effect of CL on the development of students' CT skills with reinforcement of the learners being an active pedagogy for higher academic achievement and improvement of individuals (Tsay & Brady, 2010). Development and improvement in CT are essential and can be sought through cooperative learning, and the activities help to achieve any common goal or task by a group of students (Igel & Urquhart, 2012). The following are studies regarding the development of CT skills through cooperative learning in different contexts.

A study was conducted by Nezami et al. (2013), about the effect of cooperative learning on students' CT at secondary level in the Malaysian context. A semi-experimental research design was used with randomly selected 116 students (Sixty-four for experimental and fifty-two for the control group). The experimental group was taught through cooperative learning, while the traditional method was used for control group students. The critical thinking test of Watson & Glaser (1980) was used to measure CT skills of the students containing 100 general questions with 20 questions in five factors. The findings revealed the effect of cooperative learning on CT based on gender and its sub-components, that is, comprehension, hypotheses identification, interpretation, discussion and evaluation.

A study conducted by Gillies, Ashman, and Terwel (2008) reports the effect of cooperative learning on students' academic achievement. The findings revealed that group learning and group work were productive in the development of CT skills. In the same way, cooperative learning was used for university students' language abilities and CT (Ting & Abdullah, 2020).

In the experimental study conducted by Huang et al. (2017), the effect of cooperative learning and concept mapping was examined on students' CT in basketball. It was a Physical Education class. The study was conducted with 170 respondents (Male=87, Female=83) of 5th class. The students were assigned different learning conditions: 54 with cooperative learning, 57 with concept mapping, and 59 with the control condition. The study lasted for 15 weeks. First ten weeks were for experimental instructions while the remaining 5 for retention to find out the effect of each aspect on others. Pre-test and post-test were conducted. CT was measured through 25 items questionnaires developed by Yeh (2009). The data were analysed through independent sample t-test and chi-square to find out the difference between the three groups. In cooperative learning, students improved through peer-interaction and support with team discussion for problem-solving and performance in the game; therefore, the CL method improved CT skills the most playing basketball. Similarly, Royhana et al. (2021) found cooperative learning to be an effective method for the development of critical thinking in problem-solving for 8th-grade students in an experimental study.

Collaborative Learning

Collaborative learning is a method in which students work in groups to achieve a common goal. Both individual and the group are responsible. In the process, students are actively involved through the exchange of ideas in small groups, which results in developing critical thinking. Collaborative learning might facilitate students in CT skills, where social interaction with dialogue can be seen as scaffolding. Peer interaction is beneficial during activities of collaborative learning. The students are responsible for overall as well as their work in the group.

Questioning

Questioning is an old technique which was initiated by Socrates about 2500 years ago. This technique has been proved to be useful for CT skills development among the students with problem-solving in the real-life situation since this technique has been useful for productive learning (Conner et al., 2017). Questioning plays a vital role in problem solving and creative thinking. Students may learn about the society, nature and physical aspects of the world. In science subjects, inquiry and curiosity are the essential factors for effective questioning (Ramnarain, 2011).

Questioning is considered an important aspect of developing CT skills among learners. This approach can be used to guide students since thoughtful questioning stimulates the minds of the students for probing questions to answer in a right way (Paul & Elder, 2006b). In this approach, students can exchange their ideas according to the context, exploring problems and providing a solution for their implication in a real-life situation. There have been many studies on questioning techniques to develop CT skills. For example, the use of questioning to develop CT skills among elementary level students (Rashid & Qaisar, 2016), questioning method to help develop CT skills among secondary level students (Inamullah et al., 2016), relationship of students' questioning with CT skills (Santos, 2017) and asking questioning with discussion for developing CT skills (Bevan, 2017; Khan, 2017). Conner et al. (2017) developed a module of questions for the development of CT. This module was designed for both teachers and students to play a vital role in their achievement. In the latest studies, Socratic questioning was used for the development of critical thinking in digital games (Khorraminejad, Ashayeri, Abtahi, Mohammakhani, & Soleimani, 2020). Questioning in Bloom's taxonomy levels were used to develop CT for elementary school pre-service teachers (Rahmatih et al., 2021). Following are international and national studies conducted with questioning technique for developing CT skills.

Bailey and Mentz (2015) conducted a study with the IT teachers to promote CT skills among them. They asserted that students may demonstrate and practice better CT skills in a flourishing environment. Furthermore, the students were eager and engaged with the questioning technique.

In a study conducted by Santoso, Yuanita, and Erman (2018) , the aim was to examine the relationship between students' questioning with CT skills. This was an experimental research through pre-test post-test design with purposeful sample of 94 students. A pre-test was used to check the ability of the students for asking question and CT. Then they were taught through BKBI (Bertanya Kritis Berbasis Inkuir) model (inquiry learning through critical questions). After the lesson, post-test was conducted to find progress. The results revealed that questioning had an essential role in CT skills development with inference, prediction and analysis.

Bevan (2017) explored the experiences of teachers and students regarding CT. The ethnographic methodology with grounded theory was used for data collection and analysis. Three themes were focused: cultural context and CT, classroom participation and CT, and improvement of teaching and learning through better understanding. This was a qualitative research focussed on classroom experience. Data were collected from 93 participants (42 males and 51 females) through survey questionnaires, classroom participation, poster discussion groups, student assignments and results of the examination. The questionnaires were filled in pre-course, mid-course and at the end of the course. The students were further asked to complete the assignment during the CT course. CT skills development was measured through Halpern Critical Thinking (2010) using the everyday situation and Watson-Glaser CT Appraisal short form. Questioning and group discussions were concluded to be fruitful for CT skills development.

A study was conducted by Rashid and Qaisar (2016) was designed to determine the effectiveness of questioning for developing CT skills at the elementary level. The sample of the study was fourth-grade students from three classrooms of a public school. The students observed classroom teaching and wrote field notes and pre and post questionnaires. Critical thinking questionnaire was developed to see the change before and after the intervention. Discourse analysis was used to analyse the qualitative data. The questioning strategy was proved to be productive.

In a descriptive study conducted by Inamullah et al. (2016), the aim was to find out the role of questioning for the development of CT in the classroom. Bloom's Taxonomy levels were kept in mind. The sample of the study were 176 secondary school teachers. An instrument "Observation Guide using Bloom's Taxonomy" was used. Questions asked from the teachers were recorded. Then, these questions were categorised on observation sheets according to their levels. According to the findings, it was revealed that the majority of the teachers asked lower order thinking and convergent questions through which the development of CT skills among students was not possible. Multi-type questions were recommended to promote CT skills.

Inquiry-based teaching/learning

The inquiry-based technique is a way of asking questions and finding information related to any event. Through this technique, students learn cause and effect, relationship, thinking critically as well as the combination of scientific and operational knowledge. In this way, students may use CT (Duran & Dökme, 2016). It is a productive strategy having roots in the scientific method. It may be applied to all subjects' curriculum. As an instructional strategy, it is based on an information processing model in which students are encouraged to get their meanings from different facts as well as relationships. In inquiry-based learning, questioning information is collected through findings and discussion (Cooper, 2010).

According to Orlich et al. (2012), there are different elements of inquiry-based teaching for both teachers and learners. Teachers and administrators should support this method as students are eager to find solutions through problem-solving skills. Students have to use reference books and other material for inquiry. Inquiry teaching is a process. Conclusions may be tentative since students can modify their views after collecting new data. Learners can plan, think, conduct and evaluate their effort. Administrative support is needed in all this process. Each inquiry process comprises observations, classifications, use of numbers, measurements, use of space, communication, predictions, operational definitions, formulation of the hypotheses, interpretations and control variable for experiments (Orlich et al., 2012).

Constructivism is a theoretical model which predicts how learners learn. Richardson (2003) provided a critical analysis of constructivist pedagogy with interpretation and practice. Similarities between constructivist and inquiry-based approaches have a focus on students' flexible pace of instruction, encouragement and justification for problem-solving. In this approach, students learn correlations, cause and effect, critical thinking, as well as a combination of scientific knowledge with operations. In this way, students can develop CT skills (Duran & Dökme, 2016). Through inquiry-based learning, students can acquire information and knowledge through investigation and discovery (Hwang & Chang, 2011). This approach can be implemented at different levels of problem-solving and CT skills. As compared to the traditional method of teaching, inquiry-based teaching is seen most effective for the achievement and improvement to discover information and CT skills (Blanchard et al., 2010).

Studies have showed that inquiry-based learning is a vital and essential instructional strategy for the development of CT skills. An experimental study by Duran and Dökme (2016) was carried out to find out the effect of inquiry-based learning on students' CT skills for science and technology courses at secondary level. An activity was developed regarding the inquiry-based learning approach to find out its effect in a specific unit of students' CT skills in science and technology courses.

Ninety students were selected from 6th-grade. Two designs (pre-test and post-test control group experimental) were used. According to the findings, science and technology students supported by the activities had a significant effect on the development of CT skills.

Agustini and Suyatna (2018) conducted a study to develop inquiry-based practice equipment for heat conductivity investigating the students' CT ability. Research and development method was used with the ADDIE (Analysis, Design, Development, Implementation and Evaluation) model. Students of 7th-grade were selected for field testing. The data were collected through questionnaires, observations and effectiveness of students' CT ability. For data analysis, paired sample t-test and independent-sample t-test were used. According to the results, inquiry-based practice with argument, deduction, evaluation information and using the process of critical thinking was proved to be effective in CT skills development in students. In the same way, guided inquiry method was used in a study with the main aim to find out the impact of guided inquiry method on CT skills in high school second-grade students (Azizmalayeri et al., 2012). This experimental study adopted a quasi-experimental research design with non-equivalent pre-test, post-tests. There were 190 (95 male and female each) students selected through random, multi-step and cluster sampling techniques from 8 classes. They formed four experimental and control groups. A self-developed questionnaire was used for demographic information while the Watson-Glaser test was used for evaluation of CT. Data were analysed through two-factor covariance method (ANCOVA). According to the results, guided inquiry method had a significant impact on CT skills of the students especially in the sub-scales of interpretation and conclusion. In the latest study, guided inquiry was used for the improvement of CT skills (Phonna et al., 2021).

Debates

The history of debates is as old as Greeks and was introduced about 2400 years ago. It has also been an effective teaching method for the development of CT skills. In Islamic history, it was presented in the 12th century. The debate has been a powerful and effective teaching method for the development of confidence, communication and CT skills (Hall, 2011). This method provides mind-set and confidence in reasoning for truth-seeking and thinking process (Ennis, 1993). According to Paul and Elder (2006b), the debate has six components, that is, improvement in CT, communication, guidance, development of CT with questioning, speaking skills and development of confidence.

Debates have long been used for developing CT skills (Othman et al., 2015). For example, in the Malaysian context, an experimental study was conducted by Othman et al. (2015) to find out the effect of debates on students' CT skills development at secondary level. The sample of the study comprised 40 second-language learners who had 2 hours daily activity for three consecutive days in a week. Two instruments were used for data collection, that is, New Jersey Test for Reasoning Skills (1977) to measure CT and a questionnaire comprising two sets A and B. The first instrument was used as pre-test and post-test after debates. In the second instrument, set A was given before the completion of the debate while set B at the end. The record of observations was also taken during the debate competition. The results revealed a significant difference after debate completion in the presence of CT skills.

Discussion

This method of teaching is used to explore the development of viewpoints by the teachers as well as the students. It is a very active process in which both the teacher and the student are involved (Orlich et al., 2012). Through the discussion method, students explore their opinions or perceptions regarding a specific phenomenon. Besides meaningful learning, different skills like content, attitude, skills and processes are promoted. Both speaking and thinking skills may be improved through this technique. Students' analytical skills can be enhanced through this technique, which is a source of engagement and reflection in content areas and language arts. The habit of listening should be developed in the students (Orlich et al., 2012) since it is a positive attitude and purposeful debate is impossible without good listening.

Teachers must observe the patterns of the students and support the modelling with the sound instructional practice. Group discussion was used as a teaching method to develop CT skills in students of 5th-grade (Asrita & Nurhilza, 2018). This technique is used with other techniques like questioning and practical work for developing CT skills in science subjects (Alosaimi, 2013).

Problem-solving/Problem based Learning

Problem-based learning is a method about any problem or situation to be applied with previous information to acquire knowledge. The idea of problem-solving instruction has been derived from Dewey (2004) as the major contribution from him was a curriculum based on problems and their solutions. In this method, students are given a problem-solving situation in a small group. The whole group decides to identify the information for better understanding and deal with the problem to resolve it. According to this method, with the active participation of students and self-directed learning, CT among students can be improved. Five steps are described for problem solving: problem analysis, the establishment of learning objectives, to collect information, to summarise and reflect (Lin, Chen, & Ma, 2010). In literature, the problem-solving technique is also used for the development of CT skills. Studies have demonstrated the problem-solving method used for the development of self-directed learning, communication and CT skills. In the view of Snyder and Snyder (2008), students' CT skills can be enhanced through problem-based learning. CT skills can be developed through engaging students in activities, a process for learning and assessment techniques for intellectual growth. Project-based activities encourage students for the development of CT skills. Students, in this way are users of information instead of just receivers. Kumar and Natarajan (2007) found that problem-based learning promotes CT skills, understanding learning and knowledge acquisition.

Ten steps are suggested for effective problem-solving teaching, that is to be aware of a problematic situation, identification of the problem, define all the terms, establish limitation of the problem, conduct task analysis to subdivide the problems, data collection relevant to each task, data evaluation, synthesis of data, generalisation and suggestions to rectify the problem and communication of results (Orlich et al., 2012). To encourage CT skills, ten behaviours are encouraged: plan for thinking, meaningful teaching, ask thought-provoking questions, students' awareness of the mental process by students, frequent explanation of thinking process, data before students, description by students, encouragement, consistency and patience (Orlich et al., 2012).

In the contemporary era, students are required to become problem solvers. If the students are given an assignment, they should be encouraged to do it by using problem-solving techniques, for which planning is needed. To know and how to know are the important elements of problem-solving (Orlich et al., 2012).

The teacher may play a significant role in the promotion of problem-solving method systematically. In this process, there is a problem set by the student, then the issue is clarified, required information is taken with proposed ways and then conclusions are made. Teachers should monitor the process and a written progress report is required for engaging the students (Orlich et al., 2012).

The problem-solving technique has also been used in literature for the development of CT skills. This method is proved to be useful for the development of self-directed learning, communication and CT skills. In the view of Snyder and Snyder (2008), students' CT skills can be enhanced through problem-based learning. CT skills can be developed through engaging students in activities, the process for learning and assessment techniques for intellectual growth. Project-based activities encourage students for the development of CT skills. Students in this way are users of information instead of just receivers.

Kumar and Natarajan (2007) found that problem-based learning promotes CT skills and understanding of learning and knowledge acquisition. An action research study was conducted by Chen (2015) for CT skills development through problem-based learning in media literacy. The sample of the study were 35 undergraduate students from an English class. Data collection methods such as focus group interviews, questionnaires and teachers' observations with assessment and students' writing tasks through problem-based learning were used. Qualitative data were analysed through qualitative content analysis while quantitative data with SPSS. The findings revealed PBL contribution to the development of CT with aspects of analysis, context and problem-solving. In a current study, problem-based learning was used to improve mathematical problem solving and critical thinking of fifth-grade students (Ahdhianto, Marsigit, & Nurfauzi, 2020).

Active Learning

'Active learning' is concerned with the learning through active experiential involvement of the students. It has also been a strategy for the development of CT skills. A study conducted by Kim et al. (2013) aimed at exploring the effect of active learning on enhancing the students' CT skills at undergraduate level in General Science subject. The researcher designed an active learning module. Group-based learning, scaffolding and individual reports were instructional supports. There were 155 undergraduate participants in the study from a public university. Two designed instructional modules on active learning for natural disasters were used. The implementation of each module was done for 1.5 hours with three sessions. All participants were given hand-outs and instructional material and were divided into two random groups consisting of 4-5 members. Quantitative analysis was used to explore the changes in students' CT through active learning. There was found a significant relationship between students' level of CT in their reports I and II.

Combined Strategies (Questioning, Discussion, Practical work, Dialogue, Problem solving, Examples & Monitoring)

CT skills have been developed through the usage of different combined strategies. A study was conducted by Alosaimi (2013) to explore the measurement of CT and its development in science subjects. A model of CT was developed using what, how and why questions. Based on this model, a test for CT was developed. CT skills were measured involving 240 students from both genders. For CT skills development in science subjects, 1600 students were selected for the second experiment. They were taught in experimental and control groups. Data were collected through students' perception survey, working memory test, critical thinking test and school marks. The analysis showed significant improvement in CT after using new material (discussion, questioning and practical work). Ninety-eight science teachers and inspectors were interviewed regarding their perceptions of CT in science education. It was found that it can be measured and enhanced in students through CT questions.

A meta-analysis study by Abrami et al. (2015) was conducted to find evidence from empirical studies regarding strategies for CT skills development, disposition and achievement. There were reviewed 341 true-experimental studies. According to the results, effective strategies were found both from generic and content. The evidence suggested that dialogue, problem solving, examples and mentoring had more positive effect on CT skills.

Conceptual Framework of the Study

The conceptual framework can be described as a written or visual product of explanation regarding the concepts, factors and variables and their relationship (Miles, Huberman, & Saldana, 2014). It also may be defined as the connection of variables in the study and like a map which guides a researcher for the desired investigation or location.

The main aim of the study was to analyse education policy documents and science teachers' practices for developing CT skills at the secondary level. The science teachers' perceptions were explored through an interview protocol for semi-structured interviews, and then their practices were observed through classroom observations. Therefore, the belief and practice framework was used.

Beliefs have been defined differently in the literature. These can be described as "Individual's judgment of the truth or falsity of a proposition" (Pajares, 1992, p. 316) and "As a set of conceptual representations which store general knowledge of objects, people and events, and their characteristics relationships" (Hermans, van

Braak, & Van Keer, 2008, p. 128). The term 'teachers' beliefs' has been used in the literature interchangeably for attitude, judgments, values, perceptions, ideology, disposition, implicit and explicit theories, perspectives and personal practical knowledge (Pajares, 1992). Five sources have been described regarding teachers' practical knowledge which are teachers' situational beliefs, own beliefs, experiential beliefs and theoretical beliefs (Elbaz, 1981).

Teachers' beliefs and their practices are connected since having an impact on the students' educational experiences as well as results regarding different subjects. Beliefs are correlated with practices of science teachers (Mansour, 2009). Teachers' beliefs regarding teaching-learning of science have an impact on teachers' practices as beliefs are important indicators regarding behaviours, which influence their perceptions and affect the behaviours of teachers in the classroom (Mansour, 2009; Pajares, 1992). These have been found reciprocal, but the complex correlation between teachers' beliefs and their practices both influence each other (Fives & Gill, 2014). This relationship varies based on teachers' experience, type and function of beliefs.

There is an explained relationship between beliefs and practices of teachers regarding internal and external supports and hindrances. Internal and external factors are described as the correlation between beliefs and practices. In internal factors, there are other beliefs, knowledge and experience factors. The external factors are classroom (the ability of students, their attitude, class size and classroom management), school-context factors include (parental support, administration and available resources of schools), and nation and district level factors include (education policies and curriculum standards) (Fives & Gill, 2014).

Researchers have drawn a correlation between teachers' beliefs and practices. It is also stated that these beliefs become personal pedagogies of the teachers for the guidance of practice, which play a vital role in the transformation of knowledge. For example, in the view of Poulson, Avramidis, Fox, Medwell, and Wary (2001), the correlation between teachers' beliefs and practices was found dialectical. Change in beliefs results in a change in practice (Shulman, 1986).

Beliefs and practices were also described to be influenced by cultural values of teachers and learners. Few studies showed no-consistency regarding behaviours and beliefs. However, a weak relationship between teachers' practices and their beliefs was found (Galton & Simon, 1980). This inconsistency was assumed to be developed due to some factors like classroom life, teachers' ability regarding following those beliefs and instructions according to their theoretical beliefs. This teachers' belief and practices relationship can be contradictory, a strong effect on the practice of teaching and context dependent (Mansour, 2009).

There are multiple views regarding the pedagogy of the teachers, but most are teacher-centred and learner-centred methods. Alexander (2001) has proposed an action-based framework for analysing teaching, which was used for the current study. This framework consists of three concepts, that is, frame, form and act. The following figure explains the action-based framework for analysing teaching:

Figure 2.1: An Action-based framework for analysing teaching

Frame	Form	Act
Space		Task
Student Organization	Lesson	Activity
Time		Interaction
Curriculum		Judgment
Routine, Rules and rituals		

As discussed earlier, this framework comprises three main concepts, that is, frame, form and act. The frame is composed of the context in which the teaching is conducted. There are different elements included in this aspect which are space, students' organisation, time, curriculum and routine, rules and rituals. Space is the composition of the class, students' organisation, sitting in small groups or as individuals, as well as classroom laboratories. Curriculum and time are used for different specific subjects to be covered in the allotted time. In the same way, routine, rules and rituals are composed by teacher and students' interaction during the lesson in class time (Alexander, 2001). Form aspect is the actual lesson which is delivered by the concerned teacher. The third and final aspect is the act which is formulated through task, activity, interaction and judgment. Tasks are included with learning types since that determines how a teacher deals with the transformation of knowledge, resulting in students' knowledge and cognitive development. To accomplish a task, there are different activities for the students to perform. These activities may be of different types like group discussion, inquiry methods with collaboration and debates. Through performing different activities, both teachers and students are interacting with each other through engagement with individuals and group work of the whole class. Finally, resulting in judgments, this aspect is completed. The current study used this conceptual framework for exploring science teachers' perceptions (beliefs) and practices about developing CT skills in secondary school students.

Critical Thinking Studies in Pakistani Context

There are a small number of studies conducted in the Pakistani context which argue the value of critical thinking for useful insight regarding existing issues. There is no evidence regarding developing CT in these studies; just some major issues are pointed out for the importance of CT.

For example, Ali and Buzdar (2013) conducted a study concerning reflective thinking development possibilities in distance teacher education programs at Allama Iqbal Open University (AIOU). The main aim of the study was to explore students' learning and thinking process with respect to their actions regarding habits, understanding and critical reflection. The study comprised a sample of 450 prospective teachers. The study used a questionnaire based on Mezirow's theory (1978). Findings of the study revealed a significant and positive tendency of the AIOU teacher's programs to develop critical reflection among the learners.

In her doctoral dissertation, Khan (2017) investigated CT concept within the BEd/ADE degree program in Pakistan. The study was conducted in two phases (at the beginning and end of a functional English course) to explored the facilities and barriers in developing CT according to the perceptions of the students and teachers. Furthermore, course guidelines followed for the development were also examined. A mixed methods approach (questionnaires and focus group interviews) was adopted for the sample of student teachers. Furthermore, observations of the class were taken in the courses. One hundred forty students and 7 English teachers were part of the study. Findings from first phase revealed that there was a little understanding of CT by both teachers and students. After completion of the course, it was found that teachers and students, both identified the key role of questioning in developing CT. Regarding facilitators and barriers, some identified factors by both teachers and students were the academic and social background of the students, teachers' role, classroom environment, lack of confidence and policy and practice issues. No barriers were found for developing CT skills.

A study was conducted by Mahmood (2017) to find out the effectiveness of an intervention design for the development of CT skills in an institution of teacher education in Pakistan. An explanatory mixed-methods approach was adopted. An intervention regarding CT skills was designed for a module to teach in the program of M.A. Education. Three confounding variables were the motivation of students, self-regulation and classroom learning environment. This intervention lasted for four weeks to teach CT skills. After that, a qualitative phase was conducted to explore the understanding of the intervention. Interviews and observations were used as qualitative data collection tools. An insignificant effect of an instructional intervention on students' development of CT skills was found. Motivational strategies and self-regulation had a positive impact on the development of CT skills. Different factors affecting CT skills development were the ineffective role of the teacher, the motivation of students, self-regulation and poor learning environment. It was concluded that instructions and CT skills were closely related.

There are few studies in the literature for the analysis of policy documents with reference to any specific purpose in the Pakistani context. In a study by Awan, Perveen, and Abiodullah (2018), curriculum documents were analysed for the development of CT skills in citizenship education. The study was conducted in different phases. Firstly, five elements of CT were identified from the literature. Secondly, four books, English, Urdu, Pakistan Studies and Islamiyat from secondary level were analysed. Thirdly, National Education policy (2009) was analysed regarding the particular topic. Furthermore, through the questionnaire, 100 teachers were surveyed who were teaching these subjects. The findings of the study revealed that CT for citizenship education was not focused properly in the curriculum. Similarly, a study was conducted by Arif (2011), to analyse the mathematics curriculum for class 9th with reference to its objectives, content, methodology and evaluation. The sample of the study comprised 30 curriculum experts and 1080 mathematics teachers. Data were collected through questionnaires from the teachers, while the interview schedule was used for experts. It was found that the Mathematics curriculum was not according to the demand and there was a lack of daily life examples. Activities were minimal due to which students were unable to be logical thinkers. In addition, critical thinking skills incorporated in text-based questions and tasks were explored through qualitative content analysis of the 9th grade Pakistan Studies textbook (Naseer, Muhammad, & Masood, 2020).

In the Pakistani context, there have been found two studies with respect to questioning for CT skills development. In a study conducted by Inamullah et al. (2016), the aim was to find out the role of questioning for development of CT in the classroom. The findings revealed that the majority of the teachers asked lower order thinking and convergent questions through which the development of CT skills among students was not possible. In a study conducted by Rashid and Qaisar (2016), questioning was found effective for developing CT skills among 4th-grade students of public schools.

Furthermore, another study was conducted to explore the effectiveness of an intervention design for the development of CT skills for Master-level program. There was found a close association between CT skills and teachers' professional development (Mahmood, 2017). In another context, Saeed et al. (2012) conducted a study regarding CT development through questioning in nursing. The questioning strategy was found effective in the promotion of CT skills development.

The above studies conducted in the Pakistani context, describe the nature and definition of critical thinking regarding situation and problem.

Gaps in CT Skills Development Research in Science Students

The above-reviewed literature has revealed the importance of CT and different pedagogical practices used for its development. CT skills have been much emphasized in education policy documents, national and international literature. In international literature, different pedagogical practices have been used for the development of CT skills like questioning (Inamullah et al., 2016; Rashid & Qaisar, 2016; Santoso et al., 2018), cooperative learning (Huang et al., 2017; Nezami et al., 2013), questioning with discussion (Bevan, 2017; Khan, 2017), inquiry-based practices (Agustini & Suyatna, 2018; Duran & Dökme, 2016), debates and dialogues (Abrami et al., 2015; Othman et al., 2015). Moreover, literature also provides evidence of different subjects used for the development of CT skills like in English (Bevan, 2017; Rashid & Qaisar, 2016), English, Urdu, Islamiyat, Social Studies (Inamullah et al., 2016), Chemistry (Santos, 2017), Science and Technology (Duran & Dökme, 2016).

In the Pakistani context, a small number of studies have been conducted in different aspects of CT. There are three studies in the literature analysing policy documents with reference to any specific purpose. A recent study was conducted by Rind and Mughal (2020) to analyse the Mathematics curriculum document. The main aim of this qualitative research was to get understanding of different aspects of curriculum document through discourse analysis. According to the findings, conceptual understanding was missing and teachers were not transforming knowledge according to the prescribed curriculum. In a study by Arif (2011) aimed at to analyse the Mathematics curriculum at secondary school level in Pakistan with reference to its objectives, content, methodology and evaluation. Similarly, another study by Awan et al. (2018), aimed to analyse four textbooks (English, Urdu, Pak-studies and

Islamiyat), their curriculum documents, education policy and a questionnaire from teachers for the development of CT skills in citizenship education.

There are few studies on the effectiveness of questioning for development of CT skills in the Pakistani context. For example, a study conducted by Rashid and Qaisar (2016) to find out the effectiveness of questioning for developing CT skills among 4th-grade students of public schools. In the same way, another study by Inamullah et al. (2016), aimed to find out the role of questioning for development of CT in the secondary level classroom. Furthermore, the use of questioning by educators for students' CT skills development was done in nursing (Saeed et al., 2012). Questioning strategy was found effective to develop CT.

There are also some more mix method studies conducted in different contexts of CT. The effectiveness of intervention design for the development of CT skills at Master-level program in an institution of teacher education (Mahmood, 2017) was conducted. Culture and CT, narrative from university students in Pakistan by Manan and Mehmood (2015) and reflective thinking development possibilities were explored in a distance teacher education program at AIOU (Ali & Buzdar, 2013).

The above studies reveal the importance of CT in previous literature of Pakistan, yet there is no evidence of any study to develop CT skills among secondary school students through different pedagogical practices in science subjects. Therefore, keeping in view the importance of CT in science education, focussing on education policy documents, the current government, and international literature, the current study was designed to analyse education policy documents and science teachers' practices for developing CT skills. Therefore, the current study is an attempt to address the gaps in the research literature to develop CT skills through education policy documents and science teacher enacted practices.

Summary of the Chapter

Thinking is a mental activity that relies on experience and leads toward new insights. Critical thinking is the process of thinking involving an analytical evaluation of a situation. It is a cognitive activity with the mental process. It has been defined as reflective, reasonable, independent, logical, purposeful and judgmental thinking to solve different problems. It has been described in philosophy, cognitive psychology and education. History of critical thinking dates back to Socrates, who used it as reflective thinking by application of Socratic questioning. Plato and Aristotle also used this practice. Dewey defined this pedagogical style as learning by doing. In Bloom's taxonomy, the cognitive domain of educational objectives describes analysis, synthesis and evaluation as higher-order thinking. Paul and Elder (2006c) are proponents of the current era. CT skills are the tools of inquiry categorisation, analysis, synthesis and evaluation. These skills can be developed through thinking and identifying assumption including analysis, interpretation, inference, explanation, self-regulation and evaluation looking at both sides. Scientific, creative and reflective thinking are described in the literature as types of thinking. Critical thinking has been considered as one of the twenty-first-century skills to grow "economic, technological, informational, demographic and political forces" (Bialik & Fadel, 2015, p. 4). CT has an important place in the educational context and science education regarding the development of an individual and the whole system. Science is based on hypothesis, theories and process of observation and experiments generation of knowledge. CT is the foundation pillar in science education for fostering scientific knowledge in future citizens. Critical thinking has been discussed intensively in international and national literature. The education policy documents of Pakistan focus on developing CT skills among science students with different student-centred techniques. Teachers can use various teaching strategies for developing CT skills. Four instructional approaches for the teaching of critical thinking are described in the literature as general, infusion, immersion and mixed. Critical thinking skills might be taught through questioning, cooperative learning, explicit instruction, discussion, open mind ness and decision-making progress. National education policy documents focus on developing CT skills with different student-centred techniques for the development of CT skills in science learners. Pedagogical practices for CT skills development in international and national literature are cooperative learning, collaborative learning, questioning with its different types, inquiry-based teaching, debates, discussions, problem-solving/problem-based learning, active learning and combined teaching strategies. In the Pakistani context, there are conducted few studies regarding CT skills development.

CHAPTER 3

Research Methodology

Introduction of the Chapter

This chapter consists of the purpose of research, detailed description and justification of the multiple case study research design. Moreover, this chapter describes the location and setting for research, sampling, participants of the study, epistemological and theoretical perspectives regarding data collection method and analysis, ethical consideration and procedure for ensuring the trustworthiness of the data.

Purpose of Research and Research Questions

The current study aimed to develop an understanding of how science teachers interpret and enact education policy recommendations for developing critical thinking skills among secondary school students in public schools. The overarching question for this study was: How do science teachers interpret and enact education policy recommendations for developing critical thinking skills among secondary school students in public schools?

This study was guided by the following sub-questions:

1. What are the recommendations of education policies for the development of CT skills among secondary school students in public schools?

2. What are the science teachers' interpretations of education policy documents' recommendations for the development of CT skills among secondary school students in public schools?

3. What are the science teachers' enactment practices related to education policy documents' recommendations for the development of CT skills among secondary school students in public schools?

4. What are the gaps between the education policy documents' recommendations and science teachers' enactment practices related to the development of CT skills among secondary school students in public schools?

To address the above research questions, a research design was required which could provide the logical sequence for connecting the empirical data to the study's research questions and the conclusions drawn from it (Yin, 2018). Therefore, a multiple case-study research design deemed suitable for the current study to address the above research questions. The following section elaborates the research design and provides a rationale for the selection of this particular research design.

Research Design

The present qualitative study used a multiple case study research design informed by interpretive research paradigm (Yin, 2018). The research paradigm "Constitutes the abstract beliefs and principles that shape how a researcher sees the world, and how s/he interprets and acts within that world" (Kivunja & Kuyini, 2017, p. 1). To study a particular problem, epistemological and theoretical stances are required (Yin, 2018). The current study looked into different subjective meanings of various aspects of policy recommendations, since the focus was to develop an understanding of how science teachers interpret and enact education policies recommendations for developing critical thinking skills among secondary school students in public schools. The multiple case study design was considered the most relevant for the current research, since this design offers more robust and compelling evidence than a single case study design as there is not just a single case (Yin, 2018). In-depth insight can be gained through the interpretation of cases. Through this methodology, an understanding was developed about the participants' multiple viewpoints and enactment practices for developing CT skills. Once again, the design produces the results by replicating the patterns as this provides external validation to the findings (Yin, 2013).

In the current study, a qualitative approach was adopted with an interpretive theoretical stance, which assumes the existence of the participants' multiple realities depending on their natural settings (Merriam, 2009; Yin, 2013). This approach aims at exploring the specific phenomenon in order to understand it from the participants' perspectives (Creswell & Poth, 2018; Merriam, 2009). Science teachers' interpretations and enacted practices were explored in the current case study focusing on pedagogical practices for the development of CT skills. The classroom observations were conducted to observe the teachers' practices in the classrooms with students interactions in a natural environment, where the boundaries between the object of the study and the context were not evident (Yin, 2013). It is also the in-depth explanation and analysis, regarding a bounded system, to explore a single or more cases with in-depth data collection methods like interviews, observations, document analysis, etc. (Merriam, 2009; Yin, 2013). Similar methods were used in the current study to address the research questions of the study. Furthermore, qualitative case study methodology was used because it provides a different in-depth exploration of a problem under consideration with rich descriptions and detailed explanation over a short period of time (Bell, 2014). In this study, science teachers' interpretations and enacted practices were explored through probing questions during semi-structured interviews and reflective field notes during classroom observations. This paradigm and methodology were considered suitable to get more in-depth understanding and rich results regarding the current topic.

The current study used a qualitative study approach since this approach involves an in-depth understanding within natural settings based on the words described by the participants, conducted in a natural setting and is used to get feelings, thoughts and emotions of individuals through different methods (Creswell, 2009). The main aim of the study was to analyse the education policy documents' recommendations, science teachers' interpretations and enacted practices regarding pedagogy for developing CT skills at the secondary level. In qualitative studies, the naturalistic approach is used. The classroom observations were conducted to explore science teachers' practices regarding pedagogy for the development of CT skills. Furthermore, in qualitative studies, the constructivist approach is used (Merriam, 2009) for the adoption of particular data collection and data analysis methods. Keeping in view the study design for education policy documents, document analysis was used to gather relevant data. Semi-structured interviews were conducted with science teachers to explore their multiple perspectives, and classroom observations were conducted to explore science teachers' pedagogical practices for developing CT skills in secondary level students. For data analysis, the qualitative content analysis technique (Schreier, 2012) was used since it was deemed the most suitable technique for the current study because of its emphasis on subjective interpretation—and the collected data from education policy documents required interpretation. Qualitative content analysis is the most suitable method for "Describing material that requires some degree of interpretation" (Schreier, 2012, p. 2). Furthermore, this type of analysis allows a large amount of text data to be interpreted (Mayring, 2014).

Sampling

The sample for the current study was selected through a purposive sampling technique. This sampling technique is used in qualitative studies as the research sample size is determined by the research purpose. Hence, the target population must consist of relevant individuals and according to the research purpose (Patton, 2015; Zikmund et al., 2013). The rationale to use this technique was that it identifies information-rich participants to seek understating of the phenomenon. This technique was used to fulfil the specific purpose, that is, to analyse education policy documents, science teachers' interpretations and enacted practices for the development of CT skills in secondary school students and to find the gaps between education policy documents and teachers' practices for developing CT skills among secondary school students. The sample for the study was selected from education policy documents and public school science teachers teaching at the secondary level. The following is a detailed explanation of both of the sample selections.

Sampling of Education Policy Documents

For the sampling of education policy documents, the purposive sampling technique was used since one of the objectives of the study was to analyse education policy documents (Patton, 2015). The rationale to use this sampling was to get an in-depth understanding within a particular context with reasons (purposes) for selecting specific participants, processes and events (Zikmund et al., 2013).

The following four education policy documents were selected for analysis:

- National Education Policy (NEP, 2009);

- National Curriculum for Physics, Grades, IX-X (NCP, 2006);

- National Curriculum for Chemistry, Grades, IX-X (NCC, 2006); and

- National Curriculum for Biology, Grades, IX-X (NCB, 2006).

Four education policy documents were analysed for understanding of policy recommendations regarding developing CT skills among secondary school science students. Keeping the research objectives and research questions in view, the analysis of these documents was done based on four dimensions, that is, the aim of education/curriculum and SLOs, importance of CT, pedagogical practices for developing CT skills, and assessment and CT.

Research Sites

The research sites consisted of four public secondary schools for boys from one of the districts of the Punjab province. The schools were run by the Punjab Education Department through the district provincial government as all these schools were a typical example of "Non-elitist system of education, fully dependent upon the state, and functions for the most part in Urdu" (Rahman, 2005, p. 28). These public secondary schools were from class I to class X with varying number of students. The selection of these schools was made from the official website of the School Education Punjab Government, regarding their relatively easy access (Hancock & Algozzine, 2016). The purpose of the selection of these schools was to get participants, that is, science teachers teaching Physics, Chemistry and Biology in these schools, from that specific geographical area and having a minimum of one year of teaching experience. Participants were also selected who were able to meet the objectives of the study, that is, to explore the teachers' interpretations and enacted practices for the development of CT skills in secondary school students. These interpretations and enacted practices were explored through semi-structured interviews and classroom observations, respectively. The following schools were selected as research sites.

- School A   Govt. Boys High School WWW, Faisalabad
- School B   Govt. Boys High School XXX, Faisalabad

- School C   Govt. Boys High School YYY, Faisalabad

- School D   Govt. Boys High School ZZZ, Faisalabad

Sampling of Teachers

The sampling of teachers for the current study was done through the purposive sampling technique so that information-rich participants could be recruited (Patton, 2015). This sampling technique was considered the most suitable as the main aim was to conduct an in-depth study within a particular context. Since one of the objectives was to explore teachers' interpretations and enacted practices for the development of CT skills, science teachers were selected through this technique to get more insights from the information-rich participants and to develop a more in-depth understanding of the phenomenon.

Twelve secondary level science teachers were selected as research participants through purposeful sampling technique (Patton, 2015), since this research presents multiple perspectives from diverse participants of different schools. All teachers were selected to ensure a sample of teachers teaching science subjects, that is, Physics, Chemistry and Biology teachers from four public secondary schools fulfilling the purpose of the study. In the current research, keeping in mind the perspective and characteristics of the cases, multiple case study design was used since a multiple case study design uses logic replication in which the interviewer or inquirer replicates the procedure for each case (Yin, 2013). However, to develop the best generalisations, the researcher has to select representative cases fulfilling all requirements for a qualitative study (Creswell, 2014). The participants of the study comprised teachers' teaching science subjects at selected research sites. These teachers varied by their demographic characteristics (see Table 3.3). Three secondary level teachers (Physics, Chemistry and Biology) from each school were selected as participants of the study. The following criteria were adopted during the selection of teachers:

- Teachers teaching in the selected geographical area (Faisalabad District, Punjab).

- Teachers, teaching Physics, Chemistry or Biology subjects.

- Teachers with a minimum of 1 year of teaching experience.

The selected participants of the study were as following.

Table 3. 1: Participant teachers of the study

	Public School A	Public School B	Public School C	Public School D	Total
Physics	1	1	1	1	4
Chemistry	1	1	1	1	4
Biology	1	1	1	1	4
Total	3	3	3	3	12

Twelve secondary level science teachers (3 from each school of Physics, Chemistry and Biology) were selected as the participants of the study. There were four teachers from each of the subjects from Physics, Chemistry and Biology.

An individual teacher was considered a case, which was the primary unit of the analysis (Miles et al., 2014; Yin, 2014). All the cases were bounded by a system, that is, public secondary school science teachers from one of the cities of Punjab province (Pakistan) with a data collection period. Furthermore, all cases were embedded in the political and social context of the relevant schools (Yin, 2014).

The following were the demographic information of the male teacher participants.

Table 3.1: Demographic Information of Study Participants

Teacher Code	Age (Years)	Academic Qualification	Professional Qualification	Experience (Years)	Subject taught
Phy-1.1	49	BSc	BEd	19	Physics
Phy-2.1	34	MPhil (Math)	BEd	7	Physics
Phy-3.1	48	MS (Math)	BEd	10	Physics
Phy-4.1	30	MSc (IT)	BEd	1	Physics
Che-1.2	42	BSc	BEd	17	Chemistry
Che-2.2	30	MSc (Zoology)	BEd	6	Chemistry
Che-3.2	25	MSc (Chemistry)	BEd	2	Chemistry
Che-4.2	35	MPhil (Chemistry)	BSEd	10	Chemistry
Bio-1.3	24	BS Hons (Botany)	BEd	1	Biology
Bio-2.3	55	BSc	MEd	30	Biology
Bio-3.3	36	MSc (Biology)	BEd	1	Biology
Bio-4.3	24	BS Hons (Botany)	BEd	1	Biology

Methods for Data Collection

The current section describes the methods used for the data collection in detail. Keeping in view the objectives and research questions of the study, different data collection methods were used. These methods were document analysis, semi-structured interviews and classroom observations. Data were collected through the selected four education policy documents, 12 secondary level science teachers' semi-structured interviews and classroom observations of teaching.

The following figure summarises the data collection procedures of the study.

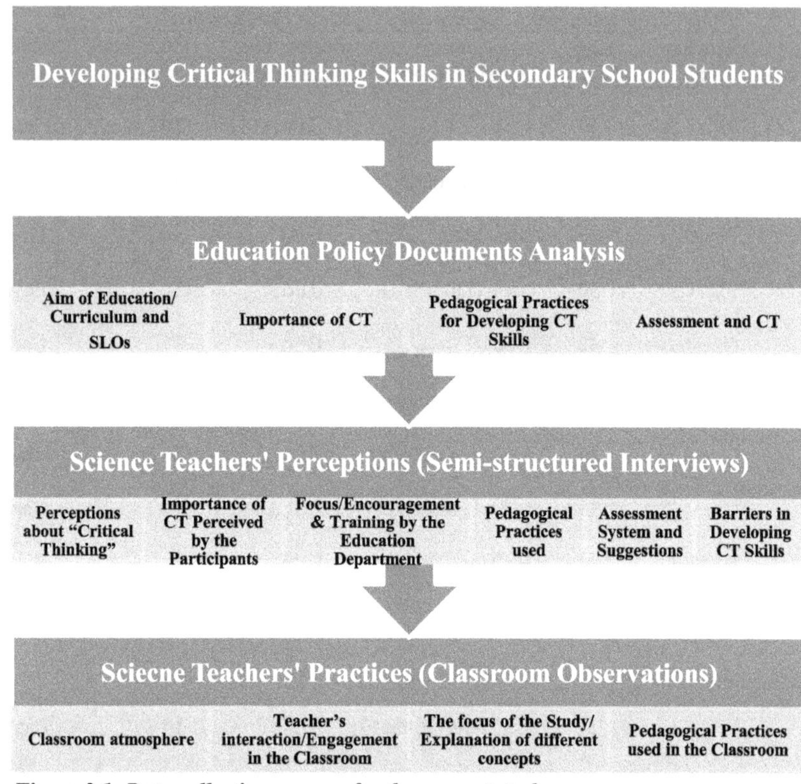

Figure 3.1: Data collection process for the current study

Each of these data collection methods is described in detail as follows.

Document Analysis

One objective of the present study was to examine the recommendations given in the education policy documents for developing CT skills among secondary school students. The rationale to use this data collection method was that it is a systematic process used for the evaluation of the documents to get meaning and understanding for the development of empirical knowledge (Muller, 2017). Furthermore, this method is primarily used in qualitative case studies to investigate a rich description of a specific phenomenon (Yazan, 2015). The following documents were analysed:

- National Education Policy (NEP, 2009);

- National Curriculum for Physics, Grades, IX-X (NCP, 2006);

- National Curriculum for Chemistry, Grades, IX-X (NCC, 2006); and

- National Curriculum for Biology, Grades, IX-X (NCB, 2006)

All four documents were analysed individually in the light of different themes, that is, aims of education/curriculum and SLOs, importance of critical thinking, pedagogical practices for developing CT skills and assessment and critical thinking.

Teachers ' Semi-Structured Interviews

Twelve science teachers (participants) were selected from four public secondary schools in order to explore the interpretations of secondary science teachers regarding policy recommendations for the development of CT skills. Semi-structured interview technique was used since it has become the most common source of data collection in qualitative studies (Charmaz, 2017) in which information is obtained by exchanging views between two persons (Brinkmann & Kvale, 2015). In the light of the research objectives, research questions and relevant literature review, an interview guide was designed. The guide was categorised into different themes, that is, perceptions about critical thinking, importance of CT perceived by the participants, focus/encouragement and training by the Education Department for CT skills development, pedagogical practices used by teachers in the classroom, assessment system regarding CT skills and suggestions, and perceived barriers in developing CT skills. Each interview opened with general and broad questions. Follow-up questions were also asked for more information to continue with the interaction. A good rapport was developed with the participants by showing respect, understanding and interest and by listening attentively.

Interviews were conducted after getting proper permission from the concerned science teachers as well as their headteachers. The research information and the interview guidelines were provided to the all participants before the interview. Since

Urdu was the first language of the teachers, all interviews were conducted in the

national language, Urdu and were audio-recorded with the permission of the

participants. After each interview, there was a debriefing session where the main

points of the interviews were mentioned, and participants were asked to comment on

them as feedback (Kvale, 1996). Recorded interviews were translated and transcribed

from Urdu to English by the researcher for further analysis. Coding and further

analysis process were done based on transcribed data in English. Since the researcher

is from the same province where the research was conducted, he was familiar with

both the culture and Urdu language of the participants. For translation accuracy, five

random transcripts were reviewed by English language experts. All ethical

considerations like confidentiality and anonymity of the participants were kept in

mind during the process involved in the conduction of semi-structured interviews.

Classroom Observations

One of the research questions was to explore the teachers' enactment practices

for developing CT skills at the secondary level. Since observations are meant to get

insights from different people in the specific context as they interact with others

(Simpson & Tuson, 2003), each of the 12 participants was observed six times while

teaching the subject in natural settings to get more authentic results. There were 30 to

50 students in each class during observations, which were video recorded. Reflective

field notes were also prepared with video recording since this was deemed a suitable

tool for classroom observations (Merriam, 2009). All possible ethical issues which

might arise during classroom observations were thoroughly considered and addressed

accordingly.

In the current study, all observations were unstructured. Mulhall (2003) suggests that an observation can be done by two methods: structured and unstructured. Prior permission was taken from the relevant participants of the study and heads of the schools. Six lessons of 35 minutes each were observed to collect the data. The role of the researcher in these observations was of a non-participant observer (Cohen, Manion, & Morrison, 2007). For the current study, the focus was on the exploration of teachers' enactment practices for the development of CT skills among secondary school students. Video recording was used for observations and data were analysed through recorded video and reflective field notes. The focus of these observations was to explore pedagogical practices for developing CT skills.

Furthermore, based on recorded videos and reflective field notes, all classroom observations were divided into different aspects of data analysis. These aspects were classroom atmosphere, teachers' interaction/engagement in the classroom, focus of the study/explanation of different concepts and pedagogical practices used in the classroom (methods of teaching, use of audio-visual aids, asking questions, problem-solving skills and cooperative learning). Video recordings were conducted by the researcher himself to capture all activities in the classrooms by concerned teachers and students.

All students and relevant science teachers were briefed about the research purpose and classroom observations. The aim was to observe the science teachers while teaching their subjects in natural settings. Prior permission of classroom observation was taken from the head of the concerned school. Concerned teachers chose the relevant lessons/lectures for the classroom observations—places where 10th-grade students were taught during the lecture of Physics, Chemistry or Biology.

To avoid the issue of trustworthiness (Cohen et al., 2007), classroom observations were converted into comprehensive reports after their transcription. Video recordings and reflective field notes were used to explore all the activities by the teachers in relation to the development of CT skills. Furthermore, at the end of each observation, reflective fieldnotes of the classroom observations were analysed through *Nvivo* 11 software.

Methods of Data Analysis

For the current study, qualitative content analysis was used for analysing data obtained through document analysis, semi-structured interviews and classroom observations. The rationale to use this method was that it is a preferred method used to describe the meaning of qualitative data in a systematic way and facilitates a detailed, systematic examination and interpretation of a particular material to identify themes, meanings and assumptions (Schreier, 2012). Moreover, it may be used for the analysis of data obtained from various sources such as documents, semi-structured interviews and classroom observations. This analysis method was used to code the data systematically for the interpretation of data collection tools like interviews, observations, field notes, etc. Furthermore, this method was used because of its three distinct features: easy data reduction, systematicity and flexibility (Schreier, 2012).

The qualitative content analysis for the current qualitative study was undertaken through *Nvivo* software version 11. This software is designed to organise and analyse the qualitative data gathered from interviews, documents, journal articles and audio-video files. It enhances the researchers' analytical capacity with efficiency. The policy documents and interpretation of semi-structured interviews consisted of many pages and the software has the ability in facilitating the process to manage, access and analyse a large amount of data (Bazeley, 2013). This is done by assigning categories to the data which may be derived from data or theory.

The text was coded and condensed to identify assertions which were linked to objectives and research questions of the study. Each education policy document was broken into small chunks or content areas and were used according to different dimensions while analysing the data, that is, aims of education/curriculum and SLOs, importance of CT, pedagogical practices for developing CT skills and assessment and CT. For semi-structured interviews, the themes were the perceptions about critical thinking, importance of CT perceived by the participants, focus/encouragement and training by the Education Department for CT skills development, pedagogical practices used by the teachers in the classroom, assessment system regarding CT skills and suggestions and barriers in developing CT skills.

Qualitative Content Analysis of Education Policy Documents

To analyse education policy documents, qualitative content analysis was used. One objective of the study was to analyse education policy documents regarding policy recommendations for the development of CT skills in secondary school science students. Four education policy documents, that is, National Education Policy (2009), National Curriculum for Physics, Chemistry and Biology, Grades, IX-X (2006) were analysed.

Nvivo 11 software was considered the most suitable to analyse the data as it provides different tools "To assist in answering the research questions from the data, without losing access to the source data or contexts from which the data have come" (Bazeley & Jackson, 2013, p. 2). There are four steps in *Nvivo* for the analysis of qualitative data, that is, importing data (files), coding data, creating framework matrices and reporting findings (Bazeley & Jackson, 2013).

First of all, the education policy documents in pdf format were imported into *Nvivo* 11 one by one as sources. Initial coding was done for concept identification. The relevant text was coded into broader areas (nodes). Then the relevant passages of investigations were sought to code in relevant nodes and child nodes which were generated keeping in view the research questions (Miles et al., 2014). This software facilitates coding the already coded data (Bazeley & Jackson, 2013). Furthermore, these coding units were summarised with the condensation process to explore in-depth meanings in the text (Bazeley & Jackson, 2013). Keeping in mind the objectives of the study, four nodes were generated, consisting of four areas of investigation, that is, critical thinking, education and CT, CT skills development and SLOs. The following screenshot, illustrates the analysis process with nodes and child nodes in *Nvivo* 11:

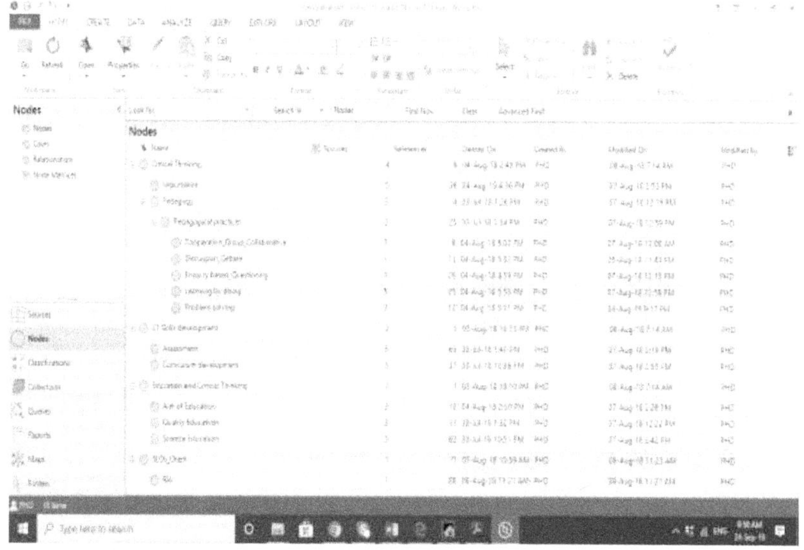

Figure 3. 2. Nodes and child nodes in Nvivo 11 for data analysis

The following are nodes and child nodes generated in *Nvivo* 11

Table 3.2: Nodes and child nodes used for Document Analysis in Nvivo

Nodes	Child Nodes
Critical Thinking	Importance
	Pedagogy
	(Pedagogical practices: Cooperative, collaborative, discussion, debate, enquiry based/questioning, learning by doing, problem-solving)
Education and CT	Aim of education
	Quality education
	Science education
CT skills development	Assessment
	Curriculum development
SLOs	regarding NEP (2009) and National Curriculum for Physics, Chemistry and Biology (2006)

Qualitative Content Analysis of Semi-Structured Interviews

All 12 audio-recorded semi-structured interviews were transcribed and translated from Urdu to English for further data analysis by *Nvivo* 11. The transcribed data of semi-structured interviews were then imported into *Nvivo* 11. All interview transcripts were read and re-read by the researcher to code for the relevant categories and sub-categories. Four nodes and their child nodes were generated, aligning with the transcribed data. The relevant passages were selected during the coding process in order to include them in these nodes and child nodes. These nodes were the introduction and importance of CT (the concept of CT, importance of CT and methods for developing CT as child nodes), focus on CT and training (focus of the department and training stuff from the department for CT skills development as child nodes), pedagogical practices used in the classrooms (activity-based, learning by doing, practical, audio-visual aids, group discussion and inquiry-based learning as child nodes), assessment system and CT and barriers/hurdles/suggestions for CT skills development. A cross-case analysis was used as this was considered the most suitable to answer the research questions (Miles et al., 2014).

The following screenshot shows the nodes and child nodes in *Nvivo* 11:

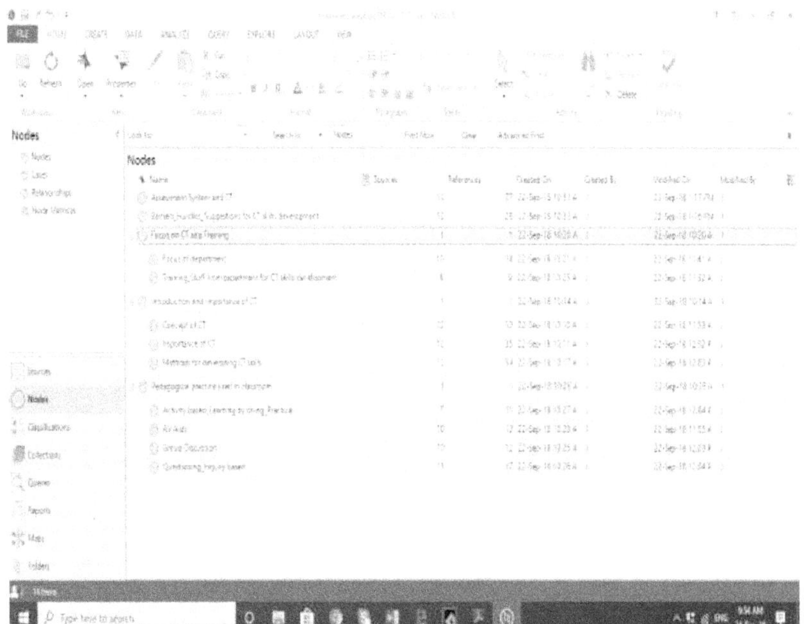

Figure 3.3: Nodes and child nodes in Nvivo 11 for data analysis

The following table shows nodes and child nodes generated for the semi-structured interviews data:

Table 3.3: Nodes and child nodes used for Interviews data Analysis in Nvivo

Nodes	Child Nodes
Introduction and Importance	Concept of CT
	Importance of CT
	Methods for developing CT
Focus on CT and training	Focus of department
	Training material from the department for CT skills development
Pedagogical practices used	activity-based, learning by doing, practical, audio-visual aids, group discussion and inquiry-based learning
Assessment system and CT	
Barriers/hurdles/suggestions for the development of CT	

Keeping in mind the research question concerning the science teachers' perceptions about pedagogy for the development of CT skills, relevant findings were extracted from the nodes and child nodes.

Qualitative Content Analysis of Classroom Observations

Classroom observations were conducted to explore the science teachers' enacted practices for the development of CT skills. Twelve secondary level science teachers (interviewed earlier) were observed. Classroom observations were undertaken through the video recording followed by reflective field notes. Analysis of the classroom observations was done based on video recordings and prepared reflective field notes, keeping in mind the relevant research questions. All field notes were imported into *Nvivo* 11 for data analysis. The relevant text was coded for the nodes and child nodes. Four nodes were generated, that is, classroom atmosphere, teachers' interaction/engagement in the classroom, focus of the study/explanation of different concepts and pedagogical practices used in the classroom (methods of teaching, use of audio-visual aids, asking questions, problem-solving skills and cooperative learning). The last aspect was the main focus of the study regarding teachers' practices for developing CT skills. Findings were drawn based on data analysis derived from nodes and child nodes.

Ethical Consideration

For the current study, ethical guidelines were kept in mind as these are standards and norms to conduct research to decide between morally right and wrong. Research ethical guidelines were considered in all phases of research like data collection, data analysis and its interpretation to seek findings of the research. In the view of Blaxter (2010), as cited by Bell (2014), the principles for research ethics have been described as follows:

> Research ethics is about being clear about the nature of the agreement you have entered into with your research subjects or contacts. This is why contracts can be a useful device. Ethical research involves getting the informed consent of those you are going to interview, question, observe or take materials from. It consists in reaching agreements about the uses of this data, and how its analysis will be reported and disseminated. And it is about keeping to such agreements when they have been reached.(Blaxter, 2010, pp. 158-159)

In qualitative research, since the researcher is the primary instrument, special attention is given to the participants' relationship, roles and status throughout the study. The researcher had to make different ethical decisions after evaluating different aspects of a social and political context where research has been conducted (Piper & Simons, 2005).

Since the data had to be collected from secondary level science teachers of public secondary schools in one of the districts of the Punjab province, it was necessary to have the permission from all the participants as well as the concerned school headteachers. All participants had been recruited from a specific geographical area. These were selected purposefully who were suitable for the study (Creswell, 2014) to provide enriched data. The researcher had taken written and telephonic consent to provide the participants' purpose of the research and briefing about semi-structured interviews. The interview date and time were fixed with the consent of the participants for their availability and comfort.

Furthermore, during the interviewing process, different steps were taken to address ethical issues. Since the participants were selected from secondary level teaching science subjects, who were expected to explore their perceptions about policy recommendations for developing CT skills, all teachers were willing to participate in the study. Earlier, they were briefed in detail about the purpose of the research.

Selected teachers had different rights in the interview process. They had the right not to answer all questions. They were free to comment or suggest regarding the phenomenon or ask questions according to their understanding. They were assured anonymity and confidentiality about them and their school. For this purpose, pseudonyms were used. All participants were free to withdraw at any stage of the study.

All semi-structured interviews were audio-recorded with the permission of the selected participants. Participants' right to privacy and confidentiality was considered, and data were not shared with any organisation or institution. Classroom observations were also conducted with the prior permission of the concerned headteachers and teachers.

Procedures for Adopting Trustworthiness

Some procedures were followed regarding the current qualitative study to analyse education policy documents and science teachers' perspectives regarding CT skills development. As in qualitative research, it is important to use the concept of trustworthiness instead of three concepts used in quantitative research, that is, reliability, validity and generalizability. As this was a qualitative study and there was no focus on generalizing the findings of the data (Schwartz-Shea & Yanow, 2013). Validation of qualitative research can be done with three perspectives, that is, the researcher's lens, participants' lens and readers' lens (Creswell & Poth, 2018). These techniques are further described as researcher lens (triangulation, negative case analysis, clarifying researcher's bias), participants' lens (member checking, prolonged engagement and persistent observation and collaboration with participants) and readers' perspective (external audit, thick descriptions and peer review). Some of the techniques are used also for trustworthiness in the following section.

Trustworthiness was dealt with in three aspects which are, credibility, dependability and transferability (Elo et al., 2014). Each of the following is detailed below.

Credibility

Graneheim and Lundman (2004) claim that credibility "Deals with the focus of the research and refers to confidence in how well the data and processes of analysis address the intended focus" (p. 109). In other words, it is seen that either the researcher has accurately represented the participants' perceptions according to their feeling, thinking and practicality or not. It is parallel to the criteria of validity in quantitative research. This aspect may be addressed in different ways, that is, the focus of the study, selection of the context, participants and approach for data collection (Graneheim & Lundman, 2004) at the level of decision making.

Keeping this in mind, relevant objectives and research questions were designed. Four education policy documents, that is, National Education Policy (2009), and National Curriculum for Physics, Chemistry and Biology, Grades, IX-X (2006) were analysed since one of the objectives was to analyse education policy documents regarding pedagogy for the development of CT skills. 12 secondary school science teachers were selected through purposive sampling fulfilling the criteria as to explore science teachers' perspectives and their practices were seen through classroom observations. Similarly, the appropriate data collection methods were used in the current study, that is, document analysis, semi-structured interviews and classroom observations.

There are four strategies to ensure the credibility, that is, prolonged engagement, persistent observations, triangulation and member check (Korstjens & Moser, 2018). In the current study, all four aspects were employed. Classroom observations were used as prolonged engagement since one of the research objectives was to explore science teachers' practices for the development of CT skills in secondary school students. For this, six classroom observations were conducted for each teacher to observe him in his natural settings. Persistent observations were also done through prolonged engagement which ensured in-depth understanding and experiences of the participants.

Regarding the current study, science teachers were observed with the main focus on their used pedagogical practices and students' interaction in the classroom for the development of CT skills. To explore the phenomenon in detail, this was done with video recordings, and later on, reflective field notes were prepared to explore relevant activities during the observed classroom. Triangulation was done by analysing education policy documents, semi-structured interviews and classroom observations as this aspect is the verification of findings through multiple sources for information and multiple methods of data collection. Education policy documents were analysed to explore recommendations for the development of CT skills; semi-structured interviews for the science teachers' perceptions and classroom observations were used for their practices regarding pedagogy for the development of CT skills. Member checking technique was also practised, as this is also one of the important techniques to establish the credibility of qualitative research. This technique was employed by letting participants review the interpretations and findings of the relevant researcher. The findings of the science teachers' interviews were shared with the participants of the study allowing them to add or edit their statements.

Dependability

Dependability aspect can be ensured through the audit trail and external audit (Creswell & Poth, 2018). This aspect involves all the explanation and process of data collection, analysis and results of the study. Qualitative researchers make this possible to be available for the review of other researchers. For the current study, the audit trail was made through *Nvivo* 11 (Bazeley & Jackson, 2013) in which analysis was done systematically. The process of data collection, analysis and results of the study were explained in detail since it involves the participants' evaluation regarding the interpretation, findings and recommendations of the study which is supported by the same data as received by the participants (Korstjens & Moser, 2018). This was also used to check the analysis procedure relevant to the accepted standards in a specific design. It describes all research steps from start to end. Education policy documents, transcription for semi-structured interviews and field notes were imported into *Nvivo* 11 for data analysis. The analytical reflection followed the coding process and categorisation of the data were taken from education policy documents, semi-structured interviews and reflective field notes based on sub-categories after identification of different themes (Miles et al., 2014). In *Nvivo*, nodes and child nodes were generated based on research objectives and research questions. External audit was carried out through a few PhD researchers after monitoring the procedure of researcher. The focus was to monitor all the data systematically since external auditor monitors the findings and interpretation relevant to the data (Creswell & Poth, 2018).

Transferability

For the current study, transferability was dealt with thick descriptions (Korstjens & Moser, 2018) and careful selection of the sample. For this study, the readers had evidence that the findings of the study would be made applicable in different situations, populations and contexts. This aspect was done by providing complete demographic information of the participants. All participants were selected through purposive sampling technique, fulfilling the specific criteria as the complete detail of the participants and setting were explained (Creswell & Poth, 2018). Therefore, to facilitate the reader, all the demographic information about the participants of the study such as age, qualification, experience and subject taught were provided for the current study.

CHAPTER 4

Data Analysis and Interpretation

Introduction of the Chapter

This chapter gives a detailed account of the findings from the qualitative content analysis of education policy documents, semi-structured interviews conducted from secondary level science teachers and classroom observations. These documents, semi-structured interviews and classroom observations were analysed through qualitative content analysis with the facilitation of *Nvivo* software 11.

Chapter 4 consists of three sections. The first section is about analysis of National Education Policy (2009), National Curriculum for Physics, Chemistry and Biology, grades, IX-X (2006). The second section comprises data analysis regarding semi-structured interviews conducted from secondary level science teachers. The third section describes the analysis of classroom observations which were undertaken to explore science teachers' practices in their classrooms. All three sections were analysed regarding the pedagogy used for the development of CT skills among secondary level science students. Qualitative content analysis was used for the analysis of data obtained from documents, semi-structured interviews and classroom observations. This method was used because it is a systematic examination and interpretation for the identification of themes, meanings and assumptions arising from qualitative data (Schreier, 2012).

Nvivo software 11 was used for the facilitation of qualitative content analysis as this software is designed to organise and analyse qualitative data, for instance interviews, documents, journal articles and audio-video files. Furthermore, it enhances the researchers' analytical capacity. The text was coded and condensed to identify themes, which were linked to objectives and research questions of the study.

With the objectives of the study in mind, four nodes were generated, and the relevant text was coded in these nodes and child nodes for further data analysis. The following sections present the detail of data analysis:

Section I. Analysis of Education Policy Documents

Education policy documents were analysed through qualitative content analysis. *Nvivo* software 11 was used for the data analysis. This software was used since education policy documents' data consist of hundreds of pages and this software facilitates a large amount of qualitative data (Bazeley & Jackson, 2013). The following education policy documents were analysed regarding pedagogy for the development of CT skills.

- National Education Policy, (NEP, 2009)

- National Curriculum for Physics, Grades, IX-X (NCP, 2006)

- National Curriculum for Chemistry, Grades, IX-X (NCC, 2006)

- National Curriculum for Biology, Grades, IX-X (NCB, 2006)

The analysis of these documents was done based on four themes, which were explored in the light of research objectives and research questions. These themes were explored by *Nvivo* software 11 through nodes and child nodes. To resolve the issue raised by research questions of the study, data were analysed through four nodes and their child nodes, that is, critical thinking (importance, pedagogy, pedagogical practices), CT skills development (assessment and curriculum development), education and CT (the aim of education, quality education and science education) and SLOs. These themes were explored through the use of Nvivo software 11 through nodes and child nodes. The following screenshot shows detail about nodes and child nodes generated in *Nvivo* 11.

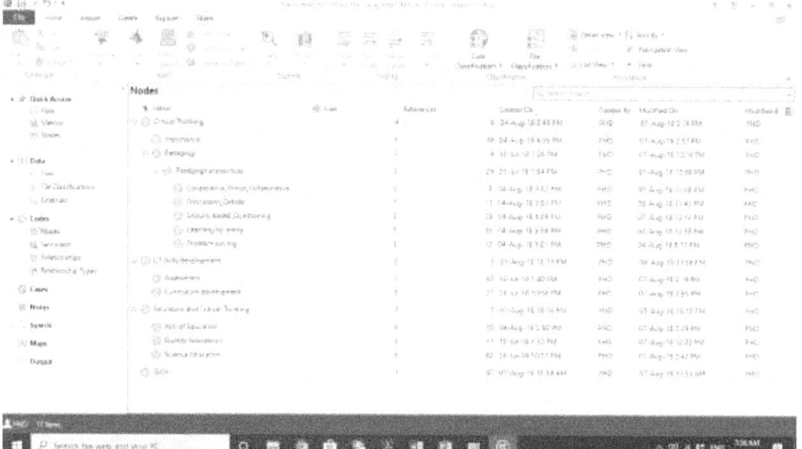

Figure 4.1: Nodes and Child nodes in Nvivo regarding policy analysis

The following is the introduction of analysed education policy documents.

Introduction about Education Policy Documents

National Education Policy (NEP), 2009 is among one of the series of National

Education Policies and Plans since 1947. Before this, the National Education Policy

(1998-2010) was presented. The review of NEP (2009) started in 2005, which

resulted in a White Paper in August 2007. There were two reasons to launch an

investigation well before the existing policy (1998-2010). First was non-production of

the desired education results and the second was due to non-completion of

international challenges regarding Education for All (EFA) and Millennium

Development Goals (MDGs).

The National Curriculum provides the framework for education in the country.

It sets directions, purpose and needs of the education, teachers' quality, educational

facilities, pedagogical practices used for the students, assessment and evaluation

mechanism. It provides the scheme of different subjects. The stakeholders involved in

the curriculum development process are policymakers, textbook writers, subject

specialists, books publishers, students and parents. The Punjab province (Pakistan)

100

adopted the National Curriculum (2006), which is the current operational curriculum. This competency and learning-based curriculum document has been designed with benchmarks, standards and students' learning outcomes (SLOs). These have been thoroughly deliberated according to the objectives of education, its significance, content, teaching methodology, assessment and evaluation process and guidelines for textbook writers. Punjab Curriculum and Textbook Board (PCTB) has launched the National curriculum for Grade IX-X (2006) for different subjects.

National Curriculum for Physics, Chemistry and Biology, grades, IX-X, were developed in 2006. All these curriculum policy documents focus and encourage the development of higher-order thinking skills among secondary school science students to become independent and life-long learners. The students are expected to think rationally and scientifically to solve their problems with decision making in their personal, social and professional lives. These curriculum documents recommend student-centred, inquiry-based, activity-based, problem-solving, group work, discussion and laboratory work type pedagogical practices for science students to develop CT skills. The following are the details of analysed data regarding four themes.

Aim of Education/Curriculum and SLOs

In all educational policy documents, the aim of education is described to develop higher-order skills in secondary level science students. In NEP (2009), the aim of education, curriculum and SLOs have been described to focus on developing CT skills for the twenty-first-century learners. To make the students responsible members of the society, critical and analytical abilities are mentioned as the aim of education. In the aims and objectives of the policy document section of Chapter 2, the objectives of education have been described as "To develop a self-reliant individual, capable of analytical and original thinking, a responsible member of society and a global citizen" (NEP, 2009, p. 19).

In the policy action section of this document, it is recommended that curriculum development should be based on objectives and should be outcome-driven. Much emphasis is given on learning outcomes rather than content. This is recommended to develop different skills and to solve social issues as it is explained in the document in the following way:

> Curriculum development shall be objective-driven and outcome-based. It shall focus on learning outcomes rather than content. It shall closely reflect important social issues; provide more room for developing the capacity for self-directed learning, the spirit of inquiry, critical thinking, problem-solving and team-work. (NEP, 2009, p. 45)

The Physics curriculum is aimed at developing problem-solving and other different skills in secondary level students. The discussed benchmarks in the documents are problem-solving through observations, reasoning, argumentation and evaluation. The aim of the Physics curriculum has been narrated as "Develop the ability to describe and explain concepts, principles, systems, processes and applications related to physics and develop the thinking process, imagination, ability to solve problems, data management, investigating and communication skills" (NCP, 2006, p. 5). A paradigm shift with interaction and participative approach has been recommended to make the twenty-first-century learners active and independent. Much focus is given on conceptual understanding through application-based investigation skills and laboratory work. Students' learning outcomes are discussed along with different factors like analysis, application and creation, with the investigation skills based on laboratory work. Standards are based on higher-order thinking skills. Benchmarks are discussed to develop solutions for problems through investigation, observation and reasoning.

The Chemistry curriculum aims at producing independent thinkers to solve real situation problems with rational thinking and decision-making skills, which will be beneficial in their practical social, personal and professional lives. It is discussed as "An ability to apply the understanding of Chemistry to relevant problems (including those from everyday real-life) and to approach those problems in rationale ways" (NCC, 2006, p. 2). Standards, benchmarks and student learning outcomes (SLOs) are described to design the current curriculum document. Standards are designed to foster higher-order thinking, in-depth knowledge, substantive conversation and connection to the world beyond the grading room. Benchmarks are created based on these standards for grades IX-X. Students are expected to display a sense of curiosity about the natural world. They must use science and technology for the identification of problems and bring creativeness into their personal, social and professional lives. It can be extracted from the document that "The aim of the Chemistry curriculum is to produce students, who will be capable of doing independent thinking, asking questions and looking for answers on their own" (NCC, 2006, p. 1). Through observations, they must generate scientific questions for problem-solving through investigation. Application and analysis are required in a number of ways in curriculum for the development of CT skills, as described in SLOs as "Describe the formation of cations from an atom of a non-metallic element (Applying) and recognise a compound as having ionic bonds (Analysing)" (NCC, 2006, p. 20).

The Curriculum for Biology also focuses on CT skills development. It can be seen through description in the document as learning at school should be based on knowledge construction with creativity for the students. On the first page of the introductory section, aspiration is described as, "To enable all students to develop their capacities as successful learners, confident individuals, responsible citizens and effective contributors to society" (NCB, 2006, p. 1). The aims and objectives for the curriculum are to make the individuals competent with logic in writing and oral presentations as well as to solve everyday life problems. It is to build the capacity of students as successful learners, responsible citizens and critical thinkers as effective contributors to society. Emphasis is given on conceptual and reasoning based study to find out the solutions to real-life problems. Learning outcomes of all of the domains of Bloom's taxonomy are discussed in depth as well.

Furthermore, this curriculum document aims to help the students in the development of scientific knowledge and understanding about the living things as aims and objectives are described in document as "Ability to apply biological understanding to appropriate problems (including those of everyday life) and to approach those problems in rational ways" (NCB, 2006, p. 1). Students must be able to learn about the interaction of living things with the environment, ask questions and use rationale strategies to recognise different scientific approaches regarding Biology for problem solving and decision making in everyday life:

> Students of Biology possess the ability to ask questions about life and can also develop solutions to problems that they encounter or questions they ask, by using their knowledge and techniques. In the process of finding solutions, students may use their knowledge and reasoning abilities, seek out additional knowledge from other sources, and engage in the empirical investigation of the living world. (NCB, 2006, p. 1)

To improve quality education, the emphasis is given to focus on different areas as described in the document as, "Improving quality requires action in the areas of teacher quality, curriculum and pedagogy, textbooks, assessment approaches, and in learning environment and facilities" (NEP, 2009, p. 42). Furthermore, the assessment system is also suggested to be revised for the promotion of quality education.

Importance of CT

Importance of CT has been discussed in all education policy documents. NEP (2009) has described CT as innovative skills, and discourages rote learning, which is a big hindrance in the mental growth. It has been focused in the policy document as "Efforts have to be made to address this issue and need for inculcating critical and analytical thinking skills for producing life-long independent learners have to be emphasised" (NEP, 2009, p. 48).

The curriculum document of Physics also emphasizes CT, focusing on in-depth conceptual understanding through problem-solving. It can be seen in the passage of identified focusing areas as "Emphasis on real-life application of concepts and problem-solving techniques" (NCP, 2006, p. 3) and "Hence, there is a need to provide the learners with sufficient conceptual background of Physics which, would eventually make them competent to meet the challenges of academic and pre-professional courses after the secondary level" (NCP, 2006, p. 1).

The importance of CT can be seen somewhat differently as described in the Chemistry curricula. It is stated that students are expected to show curiosity about the natural world and technology development. They should solve their problems through observation, reasoning and investigation. Having scientific and technological knowledge, they should become creative and decision-makers. Aims and objectives of the curriculum present the importance of CT as one of the aims is to develop the ability in the students to solve the problems of daily life by applying the rational and conceptual understanding. The standards described in the document also focus on CT skills development as they are based on higher-order thinking for conceptual knowledge with the application, analysis and evaluation.

The focus of the Biology curriculum is also on developing CT skills in students. Students are suggested to learn about the interaction of living things in Biology through questioning, problem-solving and decision-making strategies. They must be able to identify the problems, conduct and design experiments and communicate the findings by using different innovative tools. The standards have been described as higher-order thinking, deep knowledge, substantive conversation and connecting the world beyond the classroom. Scientific understanding of living things has also been described as the aim and objective of the Biology curriculum. Furthermore, one point among aims and objectives is to help the students to develop "Capacities to express themselves coherently and logically, both orally and in writing, and to use appropriately modes of communication characteristic of scientific work" (NCB, 2006, p. 8).

Different techniques are recommended for the teachers to use among students. They are expected to make their lessons interactive with different strategies to produce critical thinking as described in the Physics curriculum as "Teachers are encouraged to design their lessons in such a way that suitable questions and activities are incorporated to develop various types and levels of thinking in students, including analysis, evaluation, critical thinking and creative thinking" (NCP, 2006, p. 5).

Students are expected to have an ability of identifying, analysing and solving the problem with creativity to find solutions to problems in their daily lives as one of the standards is described as "Students will be able to display a sense of curiosity and wonder about the natural world and demonstrate an increasing awareness that this has led to new developments in science and technology" (NCB, 2006, p. 12). In the Chemistry curriculum, practical work is recommended to develop reasoning abilities in individuals.

Moreover, for in-service teachers, training is suggested through the description as "In-service teacher training in mathematics shall be given with due attention to developing conceptual understanding, procedural knowledge, problem-solving and practical reasoning skills" (NEP, 2009, p. 43). In the same way, it is described that in-service training shall cover "A wide range of areas: pedagogy and pedagogical content knowledge; subject content knowledge; testing and assessment practices; multi-grade teaching, monitoring and evaluation; and programs to cater to emerging needs like training in languages and ICT" (NEP, 2009, p. 43).

Pedagogical Practices for Developing CT Skills

In all the education policy documents, different student-centred and interactive pedagogical practices are recommended for the development of CT skills. In the policy document of NEP (2009), these pedagogical practices have been emphasized for quality education. Focus is given on the student-centred pedagogy to develop CT skills as described in the documents' policy action section, "Schools shall introduce more student-centred pedagogies" (NEP, 2009, p. 37). In the curriculum development section, the focus is to achieve objectives and learning outcomes of the students through different factors in which diverse pedagogical practices are also discussed and as described in the document as follows:

> Curriculum development shall be objective-driven and outcome-based. It shall focus on learning outcomes rather than content. It shall closely reflect important social issues; provide more room for developing the capacity for self-directed learning, the spirit of inquiry, critical thinking, problem-solving and team-work. (NEP, 2009, p. 45)

The curriculum document of Physics suggests that the student-centred interactive approaches should be used for developing higher-order thinking skills. In the policy document, it has been described as "The strategy like posing problems, discussion, investigations, and solving the problems with the involvement of the students may provide an ample opportunity in the conceptual clearance of a content" (NCP, 2006, p. 3). The emphasis is given on problem-solving techniques with the conceptual study as described in SLOs as "Developing, observing, measuring, performing and recording investigation skills/laboratory work in a context that enables students to experience the joy of doing physics" (NCP, 2006, p. 5). Different pedagogical practices have been suggested in the curriculum. In teaching-learning, there should be adopted modern techniques and methods. Students should be active learners. It is states that, "Teachers are encouraged to design their lessons in such a way that suitable questions and activities are incorporated to develop various types and levels of thinking in students, including analysis, evaluation, critical thinking and creative thinking" (NCP, 2006, p. 5). Teachers should use different techniques like questioning, problem-solving, discussion, cooperative learning, debates and students' involvement for better conceptual understanding.

The curriculum for Chemistry focuses on learner-centred, interactive, participative, practical, inquiry-based, problem solving, critical and analytical skills since the aim of the curriculum is based on developing higher-order thinking and on making the students able to become independent learners, capable of finding answers and solutions by different questions. Pedagogical practices recommended in the curriculum are learner-centred, activity-based approaches like laboratory work, demonstration, active participation, workshops, group work, inquiry-based teaching, through diagrams, flowcharts, graphs and fieldwork.

The Biology curriculum document also focuses on student-centred, inquiry and activity-based strategies for explanation and understanding as described it should be "Student-centred, assisting students in deriving their concepts from evidence and providing practical opportunities to develop individual reasoning abilities and motor skills" (NCB, 2006, p. 90). Students should be reflective and thoughtful with explanations, interpretation and applications of their acquired knowledge to gain higher-level thinking skills. In the document, there are suggested open-ended questions demanding students' creativity and critical thinking. The pedagogical practices recommended in the Biology curriculum are group work, team setting, focus on rational thinking with the formulation of questions, audio-video presentations, diagrams, graphs, flowcharts, demonstrations, investigations, debates and drawings.

For science teachers, innovative and creative teaching is recommended as NEP (2009) mentions real-life situation based pedagogy to be used during their teaching. They are suggested to use inquiry-based teaching during classes as described in the Chemistry document, teaching approaches and materials should be "Student-centred, assisting students in deriving their concepts from evidence and providing practical opportunities to develop individual reasoning abilities and motor skills" (NCC, 2006, p. 53). In the Biology curriculum, teachers are suggested to teach the process of inquiry with experience-based techniques like laboratory and fieldwork, fostering cooperative abilities.

NEP (2009) recommends training for science teachers to emphasise developing conceptual understanding through problem-solving and reasoning skills. In all the curriculum documents, in-service teacher training for professional development is recommended regarding content and methodology. The focus of this training should be based on student-centred and activity-based methods as mentioned, "Emphasis should specifically be laid on learner-centred and activity-based approaches. Laboratory practices, classroom demonstrations, active participation by the students, and field interactions should become major components" (NCB, 2006, p. 90; NCC, 2006, p. 53; NCP, 2006, p. 98).

Assessment and CT

Assessment has been discussed in the policy documents because of its influence on enactment. Analytical thinking and critical reflection should be addressed in exams. The practice of rote learning is also discussed, which is a big hindrance in mental growth and the development of CT. It has been focused as stated in the document, "Efforts have to be made to address this issue and need for inculcating critical and analytical thinking skills for producing life-long independent learners have to be emphasised" (NEP, 2009, p. 48). Such type of assessment system is emphasised, which may select or reward analytical and critical thinkers.

In the same way, different assessment tools (discussed later) are suggested to be practised, instead of traditionally used in both formative and summative assessments. In NCP (2006), CT skills development has been emphasized by the assessment system. The aim of the examination is described in the document as to assess students' different abilities for knowledge, understanding and application. Analysis, synthesis and evaluation-based questions should also be included.

Assessment has been focused on analysis, synthesis, evaluation and problem-solving. In the curriculum document of Chemistry (2006), assessment has been concentrated to examine, analyse and synthesise the information as described "Assessment should measure the capacity of students for critical judgment" (NCC, 2006, p. 55). The focus should be on students' strengths and weaknesses. All cognitive skills as knowledge, comprehension, analysis, application, synthesis and evaluations should be measured through reasoning. In Biology curriculum, CT skills have been suggested to be promoted through assessment as described in the document, "Examination system seeks a shift from content-based testing to problem-solving and competency-based assessment" (NCB, 2006, p. 1).

In all the curriculum policy documents, questions for assessment are recommended to be based on higher-order and problem-solving skills. Much focus is given to the assessment of higher reasoning capabilities of the students. The practical examination is suggested to be conducted in such a way as to explore the problem solving, daily life experience and investigation skills of the students. Students are expected to use their knowledge and skills for problem-solving. In both curriculum documents of Biology and Chemistry, formative assessment is discussed with different techniques like lab completion, worksheets, quizzes, review questions, observation, oral presentation and classroom discussion are recommended to achieve the objectives of the curriculum. In the final evaluation strategy, 85% weight should be given for knowledge, comprehension, application, synthesis and evaluation. Furthermore, in theory and assessment, 40% of questions are recommended to measure higher ability skills based on problem-solving and application of the information (NCB, 2006; NCC, 2006).

Assessment question papers reflect the curriculum; rather than textbook. Problem-solving and CT skills should be evaluated. Furthermore, questions regarding understanding, argument, explanation and the reason for the development of higher-order thinking are recommended. In policy documents, suggestions for assessment and evaluation tools are presented in the following words:

> Questions involving unfamiliar contexts or daily life experiences may be set to assess candidates' problem-solving and higher-order processing investigation skills. In answering such questions, sufficient information will be given for candidates to understand the situation or context. Candidates are expected to apply their knowledge and investigation skills included in the syllabus to solve the problems. (NCC, 2006, p. 57; NCP, 2006, p. 1)

Summary: Education Policy Documents Analysis

The four education policy documents were analysed based on four dimensions, that is, the aim of education/curriculum and SLOs, important of CT, pedagogical practices for developing CT skills and assessment and CT. Data were analysed through *Nvivo* 11. All the education policy documents aim to develop self-reliant, analytical thinkers and problem-solvers of real-life to make responsible members of the society. The focus is on conceptual understanding, investigation, application, analysis, synthesis and evaluation. To improve quality education, teachers' quality, pedagogy, curriculum, textbooks, learning environment and assessment system are suggested to be improved. Importance of CT has been emphasized in the documents to develop innovative skills and to produce life-long learners with the discouragement of rote learning. The aim and objectives are discussed, with the aim of developing the ability of the students to solve the problems of daily life by applying conceptual understanding in a rational way. Documents underscored that the students must be able to identify the problems, conduct and design experiments and communicate the findings with creativity using different innovative tools. In this regard, teachers are expected to make their lessons interactive with different student-centred strategies to produce critical thinking in students. For teachers, in-service training is recommended to consist of content, pedagogy and pedagogical knowledge to develop conceptual understanding, problem-solving and practical skills with practical and activity-based methods. Student-centred interactive approaches are recommended to be used for the development of CT skills like students' engagement, questioning, problem-solving, discussion, debates, practical work, group work and cooperative learning. The assessment system should also contain examination based on analysis, synthesis, evaluation, problem-solving and analytical thinking. Most of the assessment should focus on assessment of higher-order thinking abilities of the students. Practical examinations should be conducted to explore problem solving skills, daily life experience and investigation skills of the students. Formative assessment is discussed with different techniques like lab completion, worksheets, quizzes, review questions, observation, oral presentation and classroom discussion and recommended to achieve the objectives of the curriculum. In the final evaluation strategy, 85% weight should be given for knowledge, comprehension, application, synthesis and evaluation. Furthermore, in theory and assessment, 40% of questions are recommended to measure higher ability skills based on problem solving and application of the information. Question papers for the evaluation are suggested to be curriculum-based rather than textbook-based for the assessment of problem-solving and CT skills.

Section 2: Analysis of Semi-Structured Interviews

These semi-structured interviews aimed to explore the teachers' perceptions regarding pedagogy for the development of CT skills in three science subjects. Twelve Physics, Chemistry and Biology teachers (participants) were selected by purposive sampling technique from four schools. With the help of education policy documents and literature, an interview guide was formulated with Urdu translation. All interviews were conducted in the national language, Urdu. After conducting interviews, they were translated into English, transcribed then coded and condensed to identify themes, which were linked to objectives and research questions of the study. For the analysis of the semi-structured interviews, *Nvivo* 11 software was used. This transcribed data of semi-structured interviews was imported into *Nvivo* 11. All interview transcripts were read and re-read by the researcher to code for the relevant categories and sub-categories. Five nodes and child nodes were generated with keeping in mind the objectives and research questions of the study. The coding process was done to extract data from the transcribed text into the nodes and child nodes, which are given below:

- Awareness and importance of CT (concept of CT, importance of CT and methods for developing CT as child nodes)

- Focus on CT and training (focus of department and training material from the department for CT skills development as child nodes)

- Pedagogical practices used in the classrooms (activity-based, learning by doing, practical, audio-visual aids, group discussion and inquiry-based learning as child nodes)

- The assessment system and CT, barriers and suggestions for the development of CT skills.

The following screenshot shows the detail about nodes and child nodes generated in *Nvivo* 11 data from the semi-structured interviews.

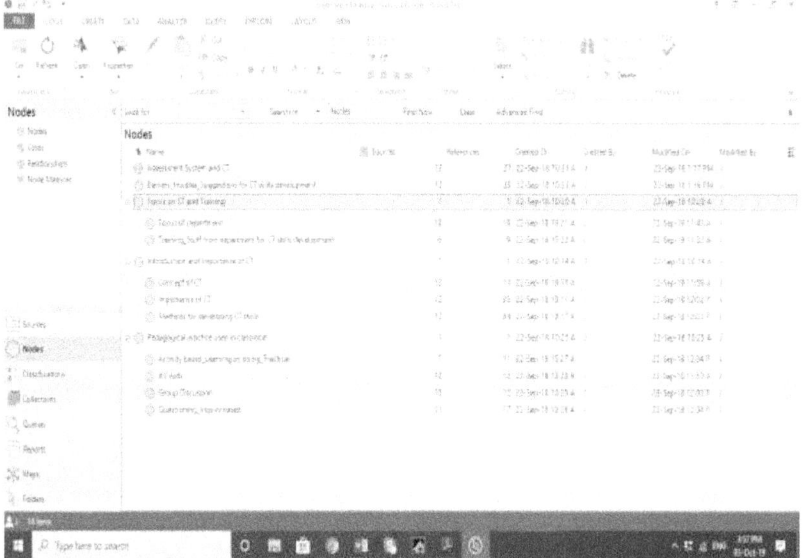

Figure 4.2: Nodes and Child nodes regarding Semi-structured interviews analysis

Keeping in view, the research question of science teachers' perception about pedagogy for the development of CT skills, relevant findings were extracted from the nodes and child nodes. Findings were divided into four sub-themes, that is, perceptions about 'Critical Thinking', importance of CT perceived by the participants, focus/encouragement and training by the Education Department for CT skills development, pedagogical practices used by teachers in the classroom, assessment system regarding CT and suggestions and barriers in developing CT skills. The detailed description of these indicators is as follows.

Perceptions about Critical Thinking

The interviewed teachers were asked to describe their understanding of the concept of Critical Thinking. All science teachers interviewed and teaching Physics, Chemistry and Biology subjects were aware of the concept of critical thinking as they defined it as a conceptual study, which develops the ability of students for developing knowledge with deep thinking, reasoning behind knowledge and to discourage rote learning. Their different terminologies and descriptions are as follows.

Most of the teachers described this concept as the development of students' ability to engage in deep thinking and conceptual based study habits. According to one teacher's understanding, it meant conceptual teaching instead of just cramming. Students should be introduced to different examples to make their concepts clear. Furthermore, it was perceived as in-depth thinking development which should be focused on teachers and students, especially in science subjects, to prepare the twenty-first-century learners as described by a teacher in the following words:

> Critical thinking is about the development of deep thought and is very necessary for students, especially in science students. Students should know how the mind works? We need to prepare the teachers and students for answering how and why type questions in which there is a need for logic and rationale. So, it is about deep thinking about any concept. (Chemistry Teacher-4)

Furthermore, CT was explained as the ability to understand any topic or concept with questioning. Another teacher considered critical thinking as the creation of different type of questions in the minds of the student about the taught topic and proper question-answers dialogue should be held between teachers and students. Students should be curious about the topic. It was described as thinking by the students by using their capabilities to learn science topics.

CT was perceived as a strategy to think deeply. It is meant to teach the students according to their cognitive ability with an understanding as it was intended by the teachers. As an interviewee explained it in the following words:

> CT is about the development of deep thinking and is very necessary for students, especially for science students. When students answer or respond after proper thinking, there will be positive academic outcomes. (Biology Teacher-2)

Some teachers described it as developing the ability of conceptual understanding among students. According to the narrative of a participant, without deep understanding and clear concepts, CT cannot be promoted. It was also perceived that CT creates the ability of deep understanding in students with conceptual study rather than rote learning, especially in science subjects. For example, a teacher described it as:

> In my point of view, students having complete understanding may learn better than only by rote learning. Students should have thinking capacity. If they are given any task, if they can describe it in their own words, it means it is critical thinking. (Chemistry Teacher-3)

The concept of CT was also described as teaching with rationale and logic by some teachers. It was also explained as teaching through reasoning as its need for the reasoning behind taught content, its solutions and implementations in practical life were described. It was suggested to develop this through learning by doing and it might be helpful for practical solutions of any tasks. One teacher described it in the following words:

> We need to teach the students in such a way that they know the reason behind what is being taught, their solutions and implementation in practical life. All this should be done with practical tasks like learning by doing etc. Basically, and science subjects demand reasoning and logic with each concept and topic. So, if

the students are taught in such a way with different relevant teaching methods and techniques, they will be better learners. (Chemistry Teacher-2)

Importance of CT Perceived by the Participants

All the interviewees were asked to explain their perceptions about the importance of CT, especially in science subjects at the secondary level for quality education. All teachers unanimously agreed about its importance for the science subjects. These included different aspects like the purpose of education, need for science subjects, decision making, facing challenges and making progress in every walk of life. Most of the teachers explained it as the purpose of education. One of the participants narrated it in the following way:

> The purpose of education cannot be fulfilled without developing CT skills in science subjects. As I explained earlier, in science subjects, we need logic and rationale for the students in teaching-learning. Therefore, there is a great need to focus on this concept and students of science subjects should be trained to answer the questions with reasoning and logic. (Chemistry Teacher-4)

Most of the teachers agreed with the view that in the twenty-first century, the purpose and objective of education should be the development of reasoning skills in students. Because of its disciplinary importance, CT skills in science subjects were considered necessary for progress in the fields of education and practical life as narrated by a teacher "Basically science subjects should be based on such activities and the objective of education should be to develop CT skills" (Biology Teacher-3). They reiterated that those science teachers should focus on conceptual based study with understanding, observation and discussion. In this way, students might develop a capability for decision making in their practical lives after having conceptual understanding which was possible without rote learning. One of the teachers stated:

> Strengthening CT skills must be the objective of education, especially in science subjects. Science, being the search for truth, is based on experiments, assumptions and their proof. It demands logic and reason behind every assumption. (Physics Teacher-1)

The importance of CT was emphasized by a few participants and they said it was a tool for enhancing quality education. It was admitted that quality education might be achieved through conceptual study and deep understanding, which were considered necessary for the development of CT skills in secondary level science students. Students' competencies for the preparation of future life were considered necessary for quality education. This was explained by a teacher in the following way:

> For quality education, these skills must be taught from the secondary level, especially for science students. To meet the educational needs and standards at international level, we must adopt techniques to face the challenges of the twenty-first century and develop such skills among students for the achievement of our goals regarding quality education. (Chemistry Teacher-3)

The importance of CT was described in different aspects for science students at the secondary level by a few participants for decision making, rationale and logical reasoning and conceptual based study habits. Teachers agreed that with the development of CT in students, they could be good decision-makers. Books only had some examples, but by giving examples from daily life they will understand better. Its importance was emphasised for success in the life of students through logical thinking. It was admitted that without CT skills, science subjects cannot be taught fruitfully. These skills were considered of vital importance to understand conceptual phenomena. It was also explained that these thinking skills must be developed among today's learners of science due to logical reasoning and thinking as basic aspects of science education learning. Because of deep thinking learning, students have a better chance to be successful in all walks of life. Furthermore, it was explained by a teacher in the following words:

> CT skills importance cannot be denied. As we say about science subjects, it should be focused concerning all different topics. Science is all about logic and reasoning; all comes through thinking skills by the students. If students are

trained from their secondary level, they will be the part of their life skills and these will be used in their decision making. (Physics Teacher-3)

One more aspect regarding the importance of CT described by few participants was competency building in the students. According to their perception, CT makes the students competent, which is beneficial for their academic and practical life. According to a participants' point of view, these skills were needed in competency building of the secondary school students; therefore, these should be emphasized. They should be taught to further understanding and conceptual based techniques, so that students might be able to explain each concept in their own words.

In the same way, CT was considered important for science students due to its use in practical life. One of the participants explained this in the following words:

> This is very important in their practical life. For example, they study the law of motion and they can apply it in their daily life by learning it practically. If the students are taught things through practice, they may use these in their life. (Physics Teacher-1)

Similarly, it was perceived important due to practical work in science subjects, which is necessary for the upcoming academic and practical life of the students. Theory and practice should go hand-in-hand for better understanding. Participants also wanted the coordination of theory and practical concepts. Due to no practical work in science laboratories, the students were unable to understand the concepts; therefore, CT was thought to be important. A teacher described the practical aspect regarding the importance of CT in the following words:

> Science cannot be proved right without implementing it in real life. I often give examples of different procedures regarding science subjects like Biology. In Biology, we may explore the flower with its different parts. Students can understand in the best way when they observe and explore it. In the same way, through a microscope, they may observe different unseen organs. And in the same way, they may understand with real life. (BiologyTeacher-4)

The importance of CT was perceived for all science subjects due to exploration through practical work and a better scientific understanding by the students. According to the perceptions of the participants, it should be required for every science subject. If students see or explore things practically, they will learn with great engagement and it will be beneficial for them. Through learning by doing, they may seek greater understanding and critical thinking. It was explained with vital importance for practical implementation as one of the teachers explained with an example in the following way:

> Critical thinking skills are compulsory in science subjects. Science cannot be proved right without implementing it in real life. Just take an example of this. Once I was teaching hydrogenation in my classroom. My students asked if they could try it at home and I said yes. The students were eager and energetic that they could start their industry if they can succeed in doing so with practical work. (Chemistry Teacher-2)

Moreover, due to having experimental methods in science subjects, its importance was admitted. Few of the participants were of the view that with experimentation, students understand the process through practical and activity-based methods, which produces reasoning and logical skills in them which are necessary for CT skills development. The following were the words of one participant in this respect:

> It is of much importance. As science subjects demand CT skills, while teaching science, the experimental method should be preferred over theoretical method to teach the high school students. These skills are with much importance for secondary school students. Science students and grade level of high school both are crucial stages for the progress of the students. In science subjects, there is a need for logical reasoning and experiments, so at this stage, when the students are mature enough to decide after taking different aspects, it has much importance. (Biology teacher-2)

The importance of CT skills at the basic secondary level for the science students was extremely crucial. At this age level, CT skills development was thought to be most useful for future practical and academic life. A participant narrated it in the following way:

> Secondary level is a very crucial stage of the students. The base of critical thinking skill is built at this level. Students learn to develop thinking and understanding at this level. So secondary level students have crucial age of

understanding; at this stage, students have a conceptual and basic understanding if teachers give them this understanding. (Biology teacher-4)

This level was considered the most suitable for concept building of the students as they learn and develop such thinking and understanding skills. In the view of a few participants, with proper training of the teachers, students might be able to do the desired conceptual tasks in the best way. One of the participants described it in the following words:

> In basic science subjects, critical thinking is very important and without it, you cannot move forward. If you have the ability of critical thinking, you will be multi-dimensional and bring new things. Otherwise, you will get marks and degrees. Especially in science subjects like Physics, in which all depends on rationale and logic. Students must be taught with such techniques which may be helpful in their future lives. (Physics Teacher-4)

In the same way, CT was considered important for the preparation of future students regarding different fields of education as well as for the progress in their practical life. It was narrated in the following way by a participant:

> At the secondary level, when students are being trained to get into medical or engineering fields, according to the twenty-first century, they need a complete understanding and conceptual based knowledge. Therefore, students must be prepared for upcoming challenges in their study as well as real life. It is of much importance. As science subjects demand CT skills, while teaching science, the experimental method should be preferred over theoretical method to teach the high school students. These skills have much importance in high school science students. (Chemistry Teacher-4)

It was explained important for innovation and future progress regarding science students as in the words of a teacher:

> They can contribute its understanding for the development of the country by innovating different types of beneficial technology. If the students know well what they are learning, they can create any invention by using their critical power of thinking" (Biology Teacher -1).

Importance of CT was narrated due to future progress in different fields and overall success in life. It was described in the following way by one of the participants:

> Yes, we need this because these students who are studying in tenth class, they will go for medical or engineering fields. Critical thinking will help them to explore many things if they know through practical or clarification of concept at

this age it will come easy further for them in their relevant fields. (Biology
Teacher-1)

Focus/Encouragement & Training by the Education Department for CT

Skills Development

According to all the participants of the study, there was no encouragement by

the department for the development of CT skills in secondary level science students.

In this regard, no refresher courses and professional development training regarding

CT skills development were arranged, and neither were they motivated by the

department head to attend training sessions. They further elaborated that no

educational officers came and motivated or encouraged them to develop of CT skills.

Rather, they had many other queries during the visit to the school. They had never

focused on this aspect nor were they encouraged to do the same to teach CT skills.

Participants were of the view that there was no inspection or monitoring from

the education department. The only focus was on results. Higher authorities and

educational inspectors had no idea about the importance of developing CT skills. One

of the teachers described the inspection of the school and its focus in the following

words:

> They (AEOs, Deputy, etc.) are mostly from arts subjects. They mainly focus on
> cleanliness, enrolment, Learning and Numeracy Drive (LND) tests of 3rd grade
> and presence of staff in school, but not on the quality of education. There is no
> interest in developing CT skills among students. They practice as usual activities.
> The monitoring system is just about different activities instead of developing CT
> skills. (Chemistry Teacher-1)

Among all the participants, one teacher was working as headteacher of the

school. He described his views according to his experience with a focus on different

aspects like attendance and cleanliness rather than CT skills development. He

explained his views in the following way:

> No, I have experience of teaching science subjects as well as heading the school.
> In my teaching practice and during my headship, I have not seen any educational

or monitoring officers, who demanded such type of creativity and skills. Usually, visitors are educational officers who focus on enrolment, attendance and cleanliness of the school. In the same way, schools are visited by Monitoring and Evaluation Assistants (MEAs) with different indicators; both of these have no such focus on developing CT skills. But in my experience, matric 9th or 10th class result is observed. If the result is below their expectations, then heads' explanation is called. So, there is no focus of the department and educational officers as well as monitoring system by the Punjab government. (Chemistry Teacher-4)

Similarly, another participant explained the focus of the officers who visited the school, focused on pass percentage of the maximum students and it did not matter whether rote learning or concept building thinking was occurring. One of the participants explained about inspection and motivation from the department and education officers in the following way:

There is no encouragement or appreciation by our higher authorities or government educational officers. The same is true from the department as well. (Physics-Teacher-2)

All the teachers narrated that they received no resources from the education department regarding the development of CT skills in their teaching experience as well as no focus of the department regarding this purpose. One of the participants presented his views in the following words:

No, Not at all. It never happened. The department of Education has not provided such type of material you are asking about. From the department, no such guidelines are received, but there is much focus on other aspects of enrolment, dropouts, attendance, etc. (Biology Teacher-2)

Furthermore, the participants were asked about any refresher course, training of professional development for CT skills development at the secondary level. All participants had not participated in specific training from the department of education. Most of the participants had received just two weeks of induction training at the start of their job, but in those trainings, there was no focus on CT skills development. The following were the views of a participant:

No such training has been conducted in my service tenure. But just induction
training of two weeks is held on every new appointment for introducing us to the
rules and regulations and information about teaching department as well as how
to deal with the students and teachers, but not focusing on CT. (Physics Teacher-
3)

Few participants reported that they had attended training, but it was based on

subject-specific like English language training at Directorate of Staff Development

(DSD) now Quaid-i-Azam Academy for Educational Development (QAED), Lahore,

in which different techniques like demonstrations and other methods were explained

to teach English subject. One of the participants told this in the following words:

In 2003, training was conducted at DSD Lahore, which I had attended for a
month. In that particular course, English for teaching was emphasised instead of
focusing on developing CT skills. Other than nothing is done in my service
regarding this type of training. (Physics Teacher-1)

Few of the participants were master trainers for specific subjects, who were

called on training in their particular subjects. They reported that the focus of this

training was not CT skills development. One of the participants was selected as

Master Trainer (Physics) to train the teachers teaching in different public schools.

QAED had organised the training courses. He described his views in the following

words:

I got trained as Master Trainer at QAED. There we are taught different practices
like these. Earlier such type of induction training was done at the start of my
service in the Education Department. But during my service period, I have not
received any specialised training, which focuses on developing CT skills among
the students. (Physics-Teacher-2)

According to the above perspectives of the participants, they had not received

any training with a focus on CT skills development. They had received just induction

training at the start of their job and some had taken training offered by DSD now

QAED during their service tenure. One of the participants explained it in the

following words:

> I attended a refresher course at Lahore DSD a few years ago. It was conducted for science teachers to teach their subject with modern technologies. Teachers from different subjects were called upon and they were trained with different new methods of teaching. But usually, there is no such type of professional development courses or training being conducted for the development of CT skills. (Chemistry Teacher-4)

Most of the participants received just two weeks of induction training on their recruitment. They did not attend any refresher course except the induction training at their first appointment. At that training, they were taught and trained about the different procedures of teaching and teaching methods. After that, there was no such training with a focus on CT skills development. According to their perspectives, the government had not arranged such type of refresher or professional development courses for the concerned teachers, especially for the science teachers to teach the students with different methods or techniques for the development of CT skills. According to one of the participants, the explanation was in such words:

> Yes, when I was appointed as a Secondary School Educator (SSE), the first time in the department, I officially attended induction training at the start of my job for four weeks. In that training, we were taught about different methods of teaching and how to deal with the students. (Biology Teacher-1)

Pedagogical Practice used by Teachers in the classroom

All interviews were conducted regarding science teachers' perceptions about their best pedagogical practices for the development of CT skills in classes. The science teachers reported that group work, discussion, questioning, activity-based, practical-based, experimental, learning by doing and audio-visual aids techniques were used in the classrooms, but the focus of these classroom techniques was not for developing CT skills among secondary level science students. The following is a detailed description of the teachers in this regard.

Teachers were asked whether they used cooperative/collaborative learning methods in the classroom. Most of them were not aware of these specific concepts;

rather, they used group work methods. Few of the teachers made groups of the students because of the large size of the class. They believed that these techniques were usually useful for conceptual study. After making groups, students were assigned tasks to complete it.

In the same way, teachers used this method to develop an understanding of the concepts with the explanation. One of the participants explained his views as follows:

> I make different groups of students to get them understand the specific phenomenon. There are students of different calibre. Through group work, they can learn in a better way. The weak students also may learn well from shining or intelligent students. Thus, this strategy is useful for science students. (Physics Teacher-2)

The questioning technique was being used by most of the participants and they believed in the importance of this technique. They used this technique to make the students curious by asking different questions about specific topic for better understanding and for clearing the concepts of all students. Such type of techniques was used to make the students attentive. The questioning method during lectures was considered very beneficial. It was being used for the preparation of annual quiz competition regarding the conceptual understanding of the students. According to one of the participants, students learn the answers themselves by using this technique as this was a very supportive technique. Through discussion and questioning, topics related to the science subjects could be taught successfully. One of the participants explained the questioning technique in the following way:

> Yes, I use questioning based techniques. This type of method is used during the lecture when there is something to be described, or there is any hidden aspect; I usually ask the students relevant questions. They are asked one by one. When they can answer the question, I appreciate them as well as motivate them when they ask questions. If there is a misconception or a wrong answer given by students, I explain the concept again and correct their misunderstanding. In my perception, this technique makes the students curious. (Chemistry Teacher-4)

One of the participants provided an example regarding the questioning technique in the following words:

> For instance, in Chemistry, when I am teaching the topic element. I ask them if water element? They reply in negative it is composed of two different elements. Similarly, I ask them if they have ever heard of enzymes. They give the example of pepsinogen. In this way, I use these techniques and have produced positive results. (Chemistry Teacher-2)

The question answer technique was being used with the lecture method technique too in a few classrooms as one participant explained that he mostly used questioning with the lecture method. This questions and answers interaction by students and teachers was helpful to get to the point of CT skills development.

Participants of the study were asked whether they used the discussion method in the science classrooms. Most of the teachers were aware of the importance of this method for better understanding of the students, but it was not used effectively because of the large class size. As one participant reported it in the following way:

> Discussion is a much important technique but seldom used in my classroom. If there are some topics which need to be explained, they are discussed. In this way, students have positive and negative aspects of the concept. (Physics Teacher-3)

Few teachers used the discussion method to clarify the concepts. According to one of the participants, students were usually given topics and asked to present these topics on board. In doing so, they were much confident and their understanding of the concept was clear. Through discussions, students' understanding of any particular topic was better. This method was being used with the questioning technique too in the classroom as described by a science teacher in the following words:

> The discussion in my class is mainly based on questions and answers session. So far, I have not practised debates and group studies techniques but look forward to doing so. For example, while teaching Chemistry, I draw the structure of the atom on board and ask my students relevant examples to build friendly interaction with them. In this way, they can understand the concept clearly. (Chemistry Teacher-1)

One of the science teachers described that he used the discussion method with traditional lecture method technique. He explained that he mostly used the lecture method, but sometimes for students' understanding, the discussion method was also used based on the topic being taught.

Some teachers reported that practical-based methods were being used frequently through which students could get a better understanding. Students could learn the concepts in the best way through learning by doing. By doing practical work, they were able to describe things by themselves. Teachers believed that practical and activity-based teaching methods were fruitful for teaching science students, since science subjects were better understood through practice. Therefore, practical work by the students might have an everlasting impact on their lives. Teachers wanted students to perform practical work, but due to shortage of practical apparatus, practical experiments were not always possible. Most of the teachers shared their experience regarding practical-based methods since these activities were beneficial for better understanding of various concepts. One of the participants explained in the following words:

> Practical-based work is necessary for understanding and conceptual study. We have limited apparatus for performing practical experiments as the department does not provide us with enough budget. Therefore, no such technique other than questions and answers session is followed in teaching theory; however, we do practical experiments and students perform them well. Practical work and learning by doing must be done for conceptual study. (Chemistry Teacher-1)

Furthermore, few teachers believed that science could not be understood or taught without practical and activity-based methods. Therefore, these techniques were used while teaching different topics. Students were asked to make charts to work more effectively. One of the participants explained his views about practical and discovery-based learning in the following words:

> Yes, in practical and discovery learning methods, students learn a lot. I use both
> of these methods because I believe that students of science subjects learn more
> with observation and practical work other than studying only theory. As a
> concern of the problem-solving method, this one is not used on a large scale, but
> whenever, there are some activities to be solved in exercises, these are given to
> the students to solve for problem-solving techniques. (Chemistry Teacher-4)

Regarding the use of audio-visual aids in the classroom, most of the teachers

explained that they used this technique with the whiteboard, charts, diagrams and

models for better understanding while teaching science subjects. They used charts and

models in science classrooms. One of the participants narrated that he used the

"Gravitation Model" in Physics for the convenience of the students. Similarly, one of

the participants described his views in the following words:

> Yes, I usually show charts and models related to any topic as an introduction to
> students in the laboratory. Due to the shortage of practical apparatus, the use of
> audio-visual aids is limited. Models are expensive and our school budget is low.
> Anyhow, there are charts in our classrooms and I try to make the students learn
> from there whenever there is any related topic. In the same way, there are some
> models which are presented in the science laboratory for clarity. Then the
> students explore them. (Physics Teacher-3)

A teacher reported that he was using audio-visual aids, charts, video clips and

models. He usually downloaded video clips for the students to show them for better

understanding. Moreover, he brought animal organs like eye, liver, etc. for physically

observation by the students and discussed in front of them. He perceived that this type

of technique was beneficial for science students.

Assessment System regarding CT Skills and Suggestions

Teachers were not satisfied with the assessment system for developing CT

skills. They believed that the current assessment system was not promoting CT skills

among secondary level science students. They asked that assessment system should

be revised with a focus on developing of CT skills. They explained that there was a

possibility of students getting maximum marks by rote learning. The type of questions

should be changed so that the students have to think and reflect on their practical life before writing the answers. One of the participants explained this in the following

words:

> The assessment of today is a demanding number game. Can you imagine that students can achieve more than 95% marks and even sometimes 100% in science subjects? Often, the questions are repeated. Besides this, the questions do not require the students to think deeply as they are bookish. In my view, when there are facts and figures based questions, they only demand rote learning. There should be how and why type of questions. (Physics Teacher-3)

Most of the participants perceived that teachers and students just emphasised

on getting good marks by memorising the topics and questions. One participant

demanded from the use of top-down approach. He further explained that teachers and

students should be ready to accept the change, and it should be implemented for the

production of critical thinkers. It was suggested that conceptual and skills-based

questions should be included for assessment to develop CT skills among students. The

participants insisted that the question papers should be based on the conceptual and

reasoning basis. Paper setters and question papers were criticised and different

suggestions were put forth. One of the participants described in the following words:

> In my view, long questions should be lessened in the paper. When the paper has been designed, it should be rechecked if it is designed according to allotted criteria. Questions regarding critical thinking must be included in the paper to assess CT skills. (Chemistry Teacher-2)

According to one of the participants, the paper setters mostly included

questions based on rote learning and repetition of questions. The students left most

questions based on critical thinking as a choice. One of the teachers demanded that

paper setters should include questions with higher-order thinking to promote CT skills

among students. One of the participants was of view and expressed his views in the

following words:

> The paper setters include questions which are based on rote learning and many of the questions are repeated in the paper. The students leave critical thinking-based questions as a choice. So, I am not satisfied with the current assessment system, because it does not promote CT skills development. Instead, there must be logical and reasoning based types of questions in the paper. (Biology Teacher-4)

One of the teachers claimed that in the assessment system, the paper does not promote conceptual based studies. The assessment system was only promoting 10 to 15% of conceptual studies. The focus of assessment and examination system was not on the development of CT skills; therefore, teachers and students just emphasised getting good marks by memorising the topics and questions.

Furthermore, according to a science teacher, the assessment system needed revision as it was not developing and measuring the desired tasks regarding CT skills development. The system does not focus on students' critical thinking, creativity and expectations to write the answer in their own words. The students prepare for the exams through some helping books, guess papers, or even there were repeated questions in the annual exams. Therefore, the system of assessment was not satisfactory with respect to CT skills development in science students. This was described by one of the participants in the following words:

> The assessment system is not up to the mark. It does not demand critical thinking and creativity in the students. Students can get higher scores in the papers. There are not many questions which are about why and how to deal with. Most are facts-based, which can be solved through rote learning. In the board examination pattern, there are not CT questions are missed out. How can we say that our assessment system is promoting critical thinking and creativity? Rather, the truth is that it is promoting rote learning. (Chemistry Teacher-3)

One of the participants gave an example regarding the formulation of questions for the assessment in board examinations. He explained it with an example as "Evaporation creates a cooling effect. How?" There is some portion of question paper which demands like how and why type questions, but due to choice in questions, most of the students do not attempt such questions.

Furthermore, it was explained that conceptual based questions should be included in the assessment system at the secondary level. There must be those questions in which students have to answer the concept behind specific questions and to enhance the quality of practical, because in BISE, the practical examination is just symbolic. Students do not perform, but get marks through the reference of their schools.

The portion of questions with critical thinking development should be increased because, in this way, students might use their minds for choosing the right option since they cannot solve paper without the proper understanding of the topic. In the same way, it was also shared by one of the participants that the students should be prepared to solve questions which need critical thinking in following words:

> To develop CT skills, the same pattern type questions should be asked, the paper should be managed and students should be prepared for exams. A major part of the paper should be conceptual based and critical based, so that students and teachers may focus on specific criteria. (Biology Teacher-2)

Overall, the assessment system is required to be revised and revisited for the development of CT skills in the question papers taken by Boards of Intermediate and Secondary Education (BISEs). The question papers were suggested to be designed with teaching questions of CT skills, which may assess secondary level science students CT skills. Therefore, paper setters should focus on including the questions needed for deep thinking assessment, creativity and developing CT skills.

Barriers in developing CT skills

Teachers were asked about the barriers they were facing regarding developing CT skills among students. Most of the teachers were of the view that the department and current assessment system had no focus on CT skills development. They believed that CT skills development was needed at that time, but there was no focus on these skills. According to a participant, the following were barriers regarding developing CT skills:

> If we are responsible for CT skills development, then there may be hurdles. There is insufficient practical apparatus. Therefore, funds should be provided to schools for developing CT skills. Students should be given prizes and motivation

to take interest in developing CT skills. It should be the department's responsibility to give awareness and importance to the teachers and promote its significance. Different audio-visual aids, practical-based activities should be included by the teachers for the teaching-learning process. In the end, if there is a demanding assessment system, then there will be effective and useful results. (Physics Teacher-2)

According to one of the participants, training and refresher courses were

suggested for the teachers' professional development and CT skills development. It was

described in the following words:

In my opinion, first, the teacher should be well trained by providing refresher courses and professional development courses regarding the development of critical thinking and should be trained with contemporary pedagogical practices, which may be useful in developing CT skills. Its implementation should be monitored continuously, before changing the assessment system according to the directions of education policies and curriculum to get positive results. (Chemistry Teacher-1)

It was also described that there was an insufficient allotted time for the lecture

and to complete the whole course. The main focus of the students was only to get

good marks and grades instead of CT skills development and interest in building

concepts. Practical facilities were not congenial for the students' participation and the

lab apparatus were outdated and broken. Practical-based and discovery learning

methods were suggested to be used for CT skills development. They suggested that

the main thing that the department should focus and concentrate on were the skills to

be developed in the secondary level science students. It was also stated that there was

a huge amount of content in the science subject, due to which CT skills development

was not focused. Unavailability of laboratory equipment, audio-visual aids and

insufficient or absence of science laboratories was explained as the obstacles. Large

classes were another factor in this regard.

Most of the participants were of the view that the focus of teachers and

students was only on getting grades and not on developing CT skills. As a participant

explained it in the following words:

Students also want to get good marks as they are not interested in building concepts. Similarly, the department wants a number of students to pass the exams. In my view, the department should focus on developing CT skills. Teachers must be ready to accept change and then the assessment system should be revised accordingly, then students will adopt such techniques to do and develop CT skills at the secondary level. (Biology Teacher-4)

Furthermore, the top-down change was recommended by the participants for CT skills development in secondary level science students. One of the participants described it in the following words:

In my opinion, if we want to develop these skills among our students, there should be a complete change starting from top-down. Education department should focus on this. Teachers should be trained through refresher and professional development courses for the development of critical thinking and should be taught with contemporary pedagogical practices, which may be useful in developing CT skills. In this way, they should teach accordingly by focusing on this phenomenon. After that, the assessment system should be changed. When these changes are made, then automatically we will get desired results. (Physics Teacher-3)

Summary: Analysis of Semi-Structured Interviews

The semi-structured interviews aimed to explore the teachers' interpretations regarding the policy recommendations for the development of CT skills in the three science subjects, that is, Physics, Chemistry and Biology. These participants were selected through purposive sampling from four public secondary schools. An interview guide was formulated with the help of policy documents and relevant literature. Semi-structured interviews were conducted in the Urdu language, which were later transcribed and translated into English for data analysis. *Nvivo* 11 software was used for the facilitation of data analysis. In the view of this study's objectives and research questions, four nodes and their child nodes were generated. Findings were divided into four sub-themes, that is, perceptions about critical thinking, importance of CT perceived by the participants, focus/encouragement and training by the Education Department for CT skills, pedagogical practices used by teachers in the classroom, assessment system regarding CT and suggestions and barriers in developing CT skills. According to the participants' understanding, they defined CT as a conceptual study, the ability of students for understanding knowledge with deep thinking, the reasoning behind knowledge and to discourage rote learning. All teachers perceived its importance for all science subjects. They explained its importance with its different aspects like the purpose of education, need for science subjects, decision making to face challenges, make progress in every walk of life, etc. According to all the participants of the study, there was no focus/encouragement by the department for the development of CT skills in secondary level science students.

The science teachers perceived that there were no arrangements for any refresher courses and professional development training for CT skills development. Participants were of the view that there was no focus of the department in this regard since no educational officers came and motivated or encouraged the development of CT skills. All the teachers stated that they received no material from the education department regarding the development of CT skills in their teaching experience since there was no focus from the department regarding this purpose. Few of the science teachers had participated in different training/refresher courses, but those were subject-specific without the focus on CT skills development. Newly recruited participants received two weeks of induction training about their teaching and other school-related information without focusing on CT skills development. Most of the science teachers used group work, discussion, questioning, activity-based, practical-based, experimental, learning by doing and use of audio-visual aids techniques in the classroom. But the focus of these classroom techniques was not the development of CT skills among secondary level science students. The selected science teachers were not satisfied with the assessment system as it was not promoting CT skills. They demanded the revision of the assessment system with the focus on CT skills development. They explained that students could get higher marks through rote learning. Conceptual reasoning and skill-based questions were suggested for assessment. The question papers were suggested to be designed by incorporating questions of CT skills, which may assess secondary level science students' CT skills. Therefore, paper setters were suggested to focus on including the questions needed for deep thinking assessment, creativity and developing CT skills.

There was no application of any technique or strategy by the teachers, department and or other stakeholders. Training and refresher courses were suggested for the teachers' professional development related to CT skills development. The main focus of the students was only to get good marks and grades instead of CT skills development and developing interest in building concepts. The schools lacked practical facilities for students' participation; therefore, practical-based and discovery learning methods and resources were suggested to be used for CT skills development.

Section 3: Classroom Observations

There were 12 secondary science teachers as participants of the study from four public secondary schools. They were observed while teaching their respective Physics, Chemistry, or Biology subjects, six times for the research. All the observations were video recorded with the permission of teachers and relevant headteachers. Students were also told of the purpose of the study and classroom observations. The main focus of these observations was to explore the science teachers' pedagogical practices for developing CT skills in secondary school students. The researcher, himself, observed classrooms by video recording. Reflective field notes were also prepared to interpret the data according to the research questions of the study. The following is the classroom observations schedule:

Teachers Observations Schedules

Table 4.1: Physics Teacher 01 Observation Schedule

Visit	Period time	Field Note Code
1	35 minutes	Phy 1.1
2	35 minutes	Phy 1.2
3	35 minutes	Phy 1.3
4	35 minutes	Phy 1.4
5	35 minutes	Phy 1.5
6	35 minutes	Phy 1.6

Table 4.2: Physics Teacher 02 Observation Schedule

Visit	Period time	Field Note Code
1	35 minutes	Phy 2.1
2	35 minutes	Phy 2.2
3	35 minutes	Phy 2.3
4	35 minutes	Phy 2.4
5	35 minutes	Phy 2.5
6	35 minutes	Phy 2.6

Table 4.3: Physics Teacher 03 Observation Schedule

Visit	Period time	Field Note Code
1	35 minutes	Phy 3.1
2	35 minutes	Phy 3.2
3	35 minutes	Phy 3.3
4	35 minutes	Phy 3.4
5	35 minutes	Phy 3.5
6	35 minutes	Phy 3.6

Table 4.4: Physics Teacher 04 Observation Schedule

Visit	Period time	Field Note Code
1	35 minutes	Phy 4.1
2	35 minutes	Phy 4.2
3	35 minutes	Phy 4.3
4	35 minutes	Phy 4.4
5	35 minutes	Phy 4.5
6	35 minutes	Phy 4.6

Table 4.5: Chemistry Teacher 01 Observation Schedule

Visit	Period time	Field Note Code
1	35 minutes	Chem 1.1
2	35 minutes	Chem 1.2
3	35 minutes	Chem 1.3
4	35 minutes	Chem 1.4
5	35 minutes	Chem 1.5
6	35 minutes	Chem 1.6

Table 4.6: Chemistry Teacher 02 Observation Schedule

Visit	Period time	Field Note Code
1	35 minutes	Chem 2.1
2	35 minutes	Chem 2.2
3	35 minutes	Chem 2.3
4	35 minutes	Chem 2.4
5	35 minutes	Chem 2.5
6	35 minutes	Chem 2.6

Table 4.7: Chemistry Teacher 03 Observation Schedule

Visit	Period time	Field Note Code
1	35 minutes	Chem 3.1
2	35 minutes	Chem 3.2
3	35 minutes	Chem 3.3
4	35 minutes	Chem 3.4
5	35 minutes	Chem 3.5
6	35 minutes	Chem 3.6

Table 4.8: Chemistry Teacher 04 Observation Schedule

Visit	Period time	Field Note Code
1	35 minutes	Chem 4.1
2	35 minutes	Chem 4.2
3	35 minutes	Chem 4.3
4	35 minutes	Chem 4.4
5	35 minutes	Chem 4.5
6	35 minutes	Chem 4.6

Table 4.9: Biology Teacher 01 Observation Schedule

Visit	Period time	Field Note Code
1	35 minutes	Bio 1.1
2	35 minutes	Bio 1.2
3	35 minutes	Bio 1.3
4	35 minutes	Bio 1.4
5	35 minutes	Bio 1.5
6	35 minutes	Bio 1.6

Table 4.10: Biology Teacher 02 Observation Schedule

Visit	Period time	Field Note Code
1	35 minutes	Bio 2.1
2	35 minutes	Bio 2.2
3	35 minutes	Bio 2.3
4	35 minutes	Bio 2.4
5	35 minutes	Bio 2.5
6	35 minutes	Bio 2.6

Table 4.11: Biology Teacher 03 Observation Schedule

Visit	Period time	Field Note Code
1	35 minutes	Bio 3.1
2	35 minutes	Bio 3.2
3	35 minutes	Bio 3.3
4	35 minutes	Bio 3.4
5	35 minutes	Bio 3.5
6	35 minutes	Bio 3.6

Table 4.12: Biology Teacher 04 Observation Schedule

Visit	Period time	Field Note Code
1	35 minutes	Bio 4.1
2	35 minutes	Bio 4.2
3	35 minutes	Bio 4.3
4	35 minutes	Bio 4.4
5	35 minutes	Bio 4.5
6	35 minutes	Bio 4.6

Classroom observations were conducted to answer the research question: What are the science teachers' enactment practices related to education policy documents' recommendations for the development of CT skills among secondary school students in public schools?

Analysis of the classroom observations was done based on video recordings and field notes, keeping in mind the relevant research question. All the reflective field notes were imported into *Nvivo* 11 for data analysis. The relevant text was coded for nodes and child nodes. Four nodes were generated: classroom atmosphere, teachers' interaction/engagement in the classroom, focus of the study/explanation of different concepts and pedagogical practices used in the classroom i.e., methods of teaching, use of audio-visual aids, asking questions, problem-solving skills, cooperative learning. The last aspect enactment, was the main focus of the study regarding the teachers' practices for developing CT skills. The following is a detail explanation according to the different aspects of analysis:

Classroom atmosphere

In summary, each classroom consisted of 30 to 50 students. The students had proper desks and chairs. All classrooms were airy with natural light and electricity. Almost all the teachers used lecture method to complete their topic in given 35 minutes. The whiteboard was used as visual aid in all the classrooms during observations. Most of the participants started their lectures by greeting with the students, writing the topic of the day on the whiteboard after entering the class. Some of the teachers asked about the topic of the day:

> Students! Which topic are we going to study today? Students chanted the topic
> aloud, then the teacher wrote it on the whiteboard. (Field note Phy 1.1)

A few teachers announced the topic of the specific day and wrote it on the whiteboard. Then they explained about its previous knowledge and linked it with the current topic. The following filed note illustrates this observation as below:

> The teacher announced the topic "Newton's Second Law of Motion". He wrote the topic on the whiteboard. Then he described some relevant terms like "Velocity" and asked the student to explain the term. One of the students raised his hand and defined the term. The teacher praised him and said "Good". Then he linked it with the topic and further explained with examples. (Field note Phy 2.1)

In the same way, another teacher announced the topic in the following way:

> The teacher wrote the topic "DNA" on the white-board and explained the students with examples of how characteristics are transferred from one cell to another cell? He also elaborated the instructions in figures and discussed the scientists who presented the model. (Field note Bio 2.6)

Few teachers asked some relevant questions from the students from previous topics and related those to the current topics as brainstorming. The students raised their hands and replied with their answers one by one. The teachers praised them for providing the correct answer and provided further explanation in case of any ambiguity or incorrect answers. Then the teachers explained each concept in detail and announced the next topic. The following field note illustrates this aspect:

> The teacher entered the class. After greetings, he recapitulated previous lecture, which was about 'What is Chemistry?' Few students raised their hands. The teacher took the answers one by one. Then he revised and explained himself. Then he announced the topic of that day. (Field note Chem 3.1)

Same techniques were used by other teachers. After completion of a subtopic the teachers usually revised the taught the content by asking students individually followed by individual explanation for better understanding of the students. As in one field note:

> Then the teacher announced the topic again for revision. He asked different sub aspects of the topic from the students and allowed them to raise their hands to answer. Some of the students answered the questions. The teacher appreciated them and announced the next subtopic. (Field note Chem 1.1)

In some lectures, different examples were given by teachers for the clarification of the content. They used the whiteboard and wrote the topics and sub-topics of the lecture on it. The following field note illustrates this concept in these words:

> The teacher used the whiteboard in the class for writing content. Topics and sub-topics were written on it while further explanation was made after that. (Field note Bio 1.6)

Most of the classrooms had a noisy environment. Due to less and little engagement, many students did not participate in the lectures. Only the students sitting in first rows seemed attentive and active, while the back benchers were busy talking to each other, thus creating a noisy environment. According to one of the field notes:

> The teacher explained the concept with examples. In the meanwhile, some of the students from the back were making noise. In front of the teacher, students were active participants; on the other hand, those sitting at the back were gossiping. (Field note Phy 3.3)

According to the observations, the noisy environment was due to less attention and engagement of the students since most of the time; the teacher remained busy in writing on the whiteboard. As per the field note:

> While the teacher was solving the numerical question on the whiteboard, some of the students from the back were whispering and doing their work, while students sitting in front of the teacher participated actively. (Field note Physics 4.1)

A few classrooms had good learning environment and the teachers played their role actively. Therefore, students were engaged in discussion and other teaching methodologies. Students sat attentively and participated in the discussion and answered the questions posed by the teacher. To start any topic, subtopic or explanation of a term, its related information was asked from the students. After the description by few students, it was further explained by the teacher through different relevant examples. Therefore, students were attentive and listening to the lectures with interest. They were also kept engaged and participative by the teachers' living

examples. Every topic was provided with different examples from daily life. In this

way, students were more participative and attentive during the class. The following

field notes give a good description:

> While defining 'Distance' the teacher provided an example for students'
> understanding. He explained it as a student going to the washroom from the
> classroom. The classroom is point A, while washroom is point B. Then he
> clarified that measurement from point A to Point B was distance. Students were
> attentive during this explanation. (Field note Phy 4.5)

In the same way, another teacher explained another term in the following way:

> The teacher described the term 'Wave'. He discussed the process of its
> production. Students were very much attentive and participative in the discussion
> and listened to the examples carefully. (Field note Phy 2.3)

Teachers' interaction/engagement in th

In most of the classrooms, there was seen less interaction among science

teachers and students because lecture method was being used. They started lectures by

announcing the day's topic. While writing the topics on the whiteboard, there was less

interaction and engagement of the students. Most of the time, teachers seemed to

remain busy at the whiteboard. Just a few students sitting in front of the teachers

interacted during an explanation of different concepts. The main focus of the teachers

was to complete the lectures with their topics and sub-topics in the provided time of

35 minutes. Therefore, most of the students remained passive and engagement

participation of students was minimum.

The scenario in this particular class was not different from the others.

Teachers used the whiteboard to write each definition, topic and subtopics with an

explanation. While writing topics and sub-topics on the whiteboard, there was less

attention of the students towards their studies. In doing so, most of the students remained passive and busy in their own activities, like staring out of the window and door and talking to their friends. It can be seen through the following field notes that:

> Sitting in front of the class, the students were attentive. Backbenchers were observed whispering. Most of the students were making noise while the teacher was busy writing on the whiteboard. (Field note Phy 3.4)

Interaction and engagement were ensured by some of the teachers in the classrooms. The science teachers used different techniques to keep their classes engaged and participative. In all these classrooms, the whiteboard was used. Different topics and sub-topics related to the lectures were written on the whiteboard for further explanation. The science teachers tried to clarify all topics with the help of different techniques. These techniques were used for the science students' interaction during classrooms. The following is the detail of these techniques:

Questioning technique was used in few lectures to keep the students engaged in the classrooms. Teachers asked relevant questions before starting any topic. They inquired from some students regarding the topic or sub-topic. The students stood up one by one and described the concepts according to their previous knowledge and understanding. After getting answers from different students, the teachers explained the concepts themselves for better understanding. The following field notes illustrate an example from the observation of a classroom:

> The teacher asked the concept from the students. Few students replied. Then he explained the concept himself with more detail and different examples involving the students by asking relevant questions and then answering those. (Field note Phy 1.6)

Similarly, during writing on the whiteboard, students participated in the discussion by answering the questions asked by the teachers. One of the science teachers used this technique in the following way.

> The teacher asked what Physics was. After taking feedback, the teacher further explained with examples. Students sitting in front of the teacher were engaged with him. (Field note Phy 3.1)

Students were also kept active and involved while solving different questions on formulas. For example, to describe the term "Salt", the teacher inquired about it. After unsatisfactory answers from the students, the teacher explained it with different examples. He also discussed the process for the preparation of salt. Types of salt were also described for understanding of the students. The teacher wrote all the relevant details on the whiteboard. Apart from this, different elements were discussed with an explanation as to how those formulas were formulated? Explanations were given by presenting various examples. The following field note describes this aspect:

> The teacher focused on another formula and was written on the whiteboard. He clarified how it was created with the combination of different compounds. With this explanation, various examples were also given for better understanding of the students. (Field note Chem 1.1)

In a few classes, teachers engaged the students by asking different questions regarding the topic. Before any explanation, the teachers asked them relevant questions from their previous knowledge and clarified them to teach the current topic. Students remained engaged and active with this act. Through the following field notes it can be seen:

> The teacher asked about the introduction of "Chemistry". Few students raised their hands and the teacher asked them to describe one by one. Each student explained the concept. Then the teacher further explained with detail by giving examples. (Field note Chem 3.2)

Similarly, one of the teachers asked the questions related to the topic in the following way:

> The teacher asked the students to describe the term "Speed". Few of the students raised their hands to explain it. Then he asked them to describe it one by one. After the students' description, the teacher explained with examples. (Field note Phy 3.6)

The questioning technique was used for the engagement of the students. Relevant questions were asked before the explanation of the concept. After announcing each idea and topic, students were asked to say something on it. Few of the students answered the questions. Further, these were clarified by the teacher himself. Such questions that were related to the topic made the students attentive and participative in the classroom. According to a field note:

> The teacher described the element of atomic no. 11. He asked the students what they knew about it. Few of them described and then further was explained by the teacher for better understanding. (Field note Chem 2.4)

During the solution of numerical questions, few of the students were engaged with the teacher while explaining the topic. They seemed to participate in the class during teachers' writing on the whiteboard. Remaining students were busy with their friends and did not pay attention to the lecture. The following field note explains this.

> Some of the students were engaged with the teacher while solving the numerical questions on the whiteboard. Some were writing the same numerical questions in their notebooks. Others were talking. (Field note Phy 1.1)

Few of the teachers engaged the classroom by keeping the students busy by asking different questions. Before starting the lesson, teachers asked different relevant questions for brainstorming and further clarification of the students. Questions were asked regarding the different aspects of the relevant topics. Sometimes at the start of the lesson or whenever it was needed questions were asked to clarify understanding. The following field note illustrates this aspect:

> Then the teacher asked, "first of all, tell me about the chemical bond". Then some of the students raised their hands to answer the question. The teacher asked them to describe the definition. The students described the definition one by one. The teacher praised on giving the right answers. Then he asked if there was anyone else for a response, but no one replied. (Field note Chem 4.3)

In a few classrooms, the teachers wrote the topics and sub-topics on the whiteboard and asked relevant question about them. Before the description and explanation of each topic, its related previous literature or linkage terms were described. Teachers usually asked the students to describe different relevant terms which they had studied in previous chapters of the book or previous class. Students were praised on giving right answers. The teachers then explained further definitions with the linkage of the current topic. In this way, students were engaged with the teacher. The following example is described as an illustration:

> The teacher announced the topic "Newton's Second Law of Motion". He wrote it on the whiteboard. Students were engaged with the teacher by listening carefully. Before starting the proper topic, the teacher asked students some relevant terms to describe like velocity. One of the students described the term. The teacher praised the students on giving the correct definition. Then he described the following definition to explain the complete definition with the combination. (Field note Phy 2.1)

Few teachers explained the topics and subtopics with detail by giving relevant examples. Students remained active and participated in the classes during the lectures by describing and discussing different concepts. Teachers used different examples for the clarification of the topics and subtopics for the students. For example, one of the teachers explained about "Gas and Liquid". He defined gas and liquid, and then he provided different examples with formulas. Furthermore, he explained the process of their formation and different terms like evaporation. He provided different examples of gas and liquid, its formation, melting process and evaporation. With the provision of examples, students remained active. One of the participants explained the characteristics of water through examples by its freezing and boiling points. He explained the formula of water how hydrogen and oxygen are mixed to produce water? Similarly, one of the teachers explained with examples in the following way:

> The teacher defined the term with complete details. After explaining the production and positivity and negativity of ions, he gave some examples related to sodium chloride. Students seemed active by participating and taking interest in the lecture. (Field note Chem 4.3)

Another teacher described "Newton's Third Law of Motion" through the example of action and reaction being equal but opposite direction, which was explained with different examples. It was exemplified by hitting a ball to the wall. One more example of the rocket was also given which travelled in the space having action and reaction process. Then another example of a balloon was given to the students to clarify the action and reaction through the reduction of air pressure.

The focus of the study/explanation of different concepts

The main focus of the study during most of the lectures was to explain the topics of that day. In almost all the classes, the lecture method was used. Teachers usually tried to complete the topic within the class time. Different concepts related to the topic were explained during the class time. On the whole, the teachers remained busy while writing topics and subtopics with their details on the whiteboard. In this process, few of the students (those sitting in the front row) took an interest in the lectures through interaction and discussion of the concepts. On the other hand, other students remained passive without noticing what was going on, and the teachers also paid little attention towards the passive students. The teachers explained the concepts and topics with different methods like the use of a whiteboard, discussion, questionings, description through examples and making diagrams. The explanation is described as follows.

Most of the teachers used the whiteboard as audio-visual aid in all the classes they taught. After announcing each topic, they wrote it down on the whiteboard, then related questions were asked of the students regarding their previous knowledge. It was also helpful in engaging the students in the class. Students were given a chance to provide their feedback about the concerned topics. Then they were further explained by teachers properly with the linking of the previous topic and steps of the current topic. The following example from a field note describes it in these words:

> The teacher wrote the formula on the whiteboard. He explained how it was formulated with division and multiply process. Students were engaged and were listening attentively to the teacher. (Field note Phy 1.6)

Most of the teachers used the whiteboard during classes for writing the related text of topics and subtopics. Students were engaged in the classrooms while writing these topics on the whiteboard. Teachers asked questions related to the previous topics. The students raised their hands and gave the right answers. These topics were further explained by the teacher. The focus of these concepts was for further understanding of the students. In some of the lectures, if there was any ambiguity in explanation of topics and subtopics, they were further clarified with examples by the teachers. The following field note describes this aspect as under:

> The teacher completed the topics and its sub topics with an explanation. Then started the session for further explanation. After clarification, these were revised by asking students the relevant questions. (Field note Chem 3.2)

The whiteboard was used in most of the classrooms. A few of the teachers wrote the topics on the whiteboard on starting the lectures. Afterwards, students were asked relevant questions from their previous knowledge and the teacher correlated the current topic with the previous lecture. Further explanation was given with details. Through this method, students were active and their participation in the lectures was visible. According to a field note:

> The teacher used whiteboard. After writing the topic, it was described and explained. Earlier, relevant questions were also asked by the students. Students provided feedback and then further explanation was made by the teacher. (Field note Bio 4.6)

The whiteboard was used for writing the topics, subtopics and different aspects. Teachers wrote the topics on the whiteboard. Then they asked relevant questions from the students as a brainstorming technique. After eliciting their previous knowledge, they explained the topics written on the whiteboard and further explained. This practice made the students alert and they participated during the lectures by listening attentively. According to the following field note, it may be seen:

The students were attentive throughout the lecture and paid attention on what
was written on the whiteboard. Further, he explained these concepts. Students
were engaged while discussing and asking questions. (Field note Bio 1.5)

The whiteboard was used to solve numerical questions too by one of the

teachers. He made the students participate in the lecture while answering questions.

Students were introduced to the concept of problem-solving technique and it was used

by them later to solve different numerical questions. Most of the students were

passive sitting at the back, while the teacher was solving different numerical questions

on the whiteboard. Teachers' interaction was with the students who were sitting in

front as they were participating during the solution of the questions.

In a few classroom observations, questioning was used in different parts of the

lectures. Questions were asked at various points: before the lecture started, while the

lecture was being given and after the lecture. Students were observed to be active

during this practice. Relevant questions were asked from the students one by one and

were praised on giving the right answers, which were explained for further

clarification. While revising the lecture, these questions were also asked by the

teacher so that students could understand the concepts in a better way. Through

questioning, students remained engaged and active during classroom lectures. In the

following field note, this aspect is captured:

The teacher asked about the concept. Some of the students raised their hands. He
provided them with feedback and praised on their explanation and then explained
by the teacher further (Field note Chem 4.5)

The teachers usually explained the concepts on the whiteboard by using the

questioning technique. In this way, the students were kept engaged in the classrooms.

According to the following field note, it may be explained that:

The teacher announced the topic "Ultrasound Waves". It was written on the
whiteboard. Students were asked about waves. The teacher asked different
questions related to the topic. Students were kept engaged by thinking and

answering to the questioning. After having a response from the students, the
teacher further explained the topics. (Field note Phy 2.3)

The concepts were clarified through asking relevant questions at the start of
the lesson. One of the teachers inquired about the concept before starting to explain.
After listening to the answers, he further explained the concept. For example, on the
topic of controlling air pollution, the teacher asked the students to provide an idea to
control air pollution. On providing the right answer, the teacher praised the students.
On the other hand, he made corrections when the answers were not correct. Then he
explained the concept with details to make it understandable for the students.

Few teachers explained different concepts with complete details through
proper relevant examples. The technique that supported the students' engagement was
the provision of different living relevant examples from the surroundings. The
students remained active and they participated in the discussion while understanding
the taught topics. The following field note illustrates this aspect:

> While describing the notion of action and reaction, the teacher provided different
> examples like hitting the ball, rocket and air in the balloon. In all examples, the
> teacher explained how action and reaction worked. (Field note Phy 2.3)

The concepts were also explained through examples provided by the teacher.
The students were active and listened to the lectures carefully during this practice. For
example, one of the participants started teaching a topic. First of all, he described it
with all details and then provided relevant examples for more understanding of the
specific concept. While describing the process of "Mitosis", the teacher explained its
different stages with the help of examples for the students.

Similarly, more concepts were explained through the provision of different
relevant examples, thus, the students were able to understand the specific topic in a
better way. The following field note illustrates this aspect:

The teacher explained the term after the describing in detail. After that, he
presented how positive and negative ions produced. Some relevant examples
were also given for the clarification of the topic. (Field note Chem 4.2)

In some cases, the teachers used some living examples too from the daily life
of the students for their understanding. For example, while describing the formulas
like NaCl, one of the participants explained how both sodium and chlorine were
combined and salt was created.

One of the teachers also used examples from daily life. The students took
great interest and were active in learning throughout the class time. The teacher gave
an example "Clean Green Pakistan" regarding how to minimise air pollution as this
slogan was being used by the government to reduce pollution and keep the
environment clean. In the same way, he also elaborated "Zigzag" technology
introduced by the government to minimise the air pollution by plugging in the
chimney of the brick kiln.

A positive aspect during the lectures was the revision of the topics in the
classrooms by few of the teachers. In this way, students became attentive and
participative in the lectures as they had to explain the topic which had been taught so
far. Furthermore, these were explained again for a clear understanding of the students.
The following field note illustrates this aspect:

> After the completion of the whole lecture, teacher revised the concepts discussed
> by asking the students. (Field note Chem 3.5)

Few teachers revised and summarized the whole topic at the end of the lecture.
They clarified the topics and subtopics followed by different relevant questions from
the students. According to the following field note, it can be observed:

> The teacher also revised various taught aspects of the topic at the end. To
> accomplish this, the teacher asked questions regarding the different taught
> concepts. They were asked to describe their perceptions they had developed
> during the lecture. Students recalled and described the concepts one by one.
> Some of the students were asked to come to the whiteboard to explain the

concepts. If anyone hesitated during explanation, these were further explained by
the teacher. (Field note Bio 3.4)

Few teachers used the whiteboard for students as they called the students to
come and asked them to describe the concept. In this way, students were attentive and
engaged. As in the view of the following field note:

> One of the students was asked to write on the whiteboard according to the
> instructions of the teacher. The student came and wrote the description of the
> term on the whiteboard. Then the teacher explained the concept further with an
> example. (Field note Chem 1.3)

Few of the teachers used diagrams for developing an understanding of the
students. After writing the topics on the whiteboard, their description and explanation,
and diagrams were made. One of the Biology teachers made a diagram of the cell on
the whiteboard and then he described and explained its different aspects in detail by
pointing towards them. In the same way, the following field note illustrates this
aspect.

> The teacher made a diagram on the white-board do describe "DNA". He pointed
> to the whiteboard for further explanation with examples Fieldnote Bio 2.6)

***Pedagogical practices used in the classroom (Methods of teaching, use of
audio-visual aids, asking questions, problem-solving skills, cooperative
learning)***

It was observed in all classrooms that there was no special focus on
pedagogical practices for the development of CT skills among science students. In
almost all the classes, lecture method was used without proper engagement and
participation of the students. The whiteboard was used in all the lectures as a visual
aid to write the topics, subtopics, solve numerical questions and diagrams. Some other
techniques like questioning, using examples, discussion and diagrams were also used
during the lectures. Details of these techniques are as follows:

Almost all the participants used the whiteboard during all the lectures. It was used to write the taught topics, subtopics and explanation of different aspects. Teachers explained them by pointing towards the whiteboard for students understanding. The students sitting in front of the teachers were engaged and participated during the lecture. According to the following field note, it is illustrated in these words:

> After the announcement of the topic, the teacher wrote it on the whiteboard. For the attention of the students, he explained the concept with detail for them to understand and participate. (Field note Phy 1.6)

The whiteboard was also used for the solution and explanation of formulas. According to a Physics teachers' methodology, he explained formulas on the whiteboard and most of the students remained passive, while few were engaged.

In the same way, the chemistry teacher wrote the concept on the whiteboard and then asked the students to describe it. Few of the students explained according to their understanding. Then he further pointed to the whiteboard and explained the concept in detail.

In most of the classes, students focussed on the whiteboard as they were interacting with the teachers and seemed to be active in the classrooms. After announcing the topic, the teachers wrote on the whiteboard. Then they started to describe it and presented its explanation while engaging the students with them. In discussing different topics on the whiteboard, relevant questions were asked from the students and the teachers made the explanation for a clear understanding of the students. Charts were also used to indicate different aspects of taught topics and then the teachers explained these with examples. The following field note illustrates:

> The teacher announced the topic "Types of Chemistry" wrote on the whiteboard and then described its types. Furthermore, he explained it from the chart to point out different types and their usage in practical life. Students were listening very attentively and were engaged with the teacher. (Field note Chem 3.1).

Some teachers also used the questioning technique during the lessons in different ways. Questions were used at the start of the lecture for brainstorming and for checking the previous knowledge of the students, while discussing and explaining different concepts and sub-concepts and finally at the end of the lectures while revising the same.

The questioning technique was used in few lectures for brainstorming, complete understanding and preparation for that day's topic. Students remained active and engaged during this practice. This was done to check the previous knowledge of the students about the specific topic. In some classrooms, students were expected to answer question; therefore, all were attentive and took an interest in the lectures. In this regard, some relevant issues of the topics were asked by the students. Then they were further explained with different examples. According to an observation of a Biology teacher, he talked about 'Transportation' and discussed the 'Circulation of Blood'. He asked some relevant questions related to blood groups and their diseases. Few of the students answered according to their understanding. Then the teacher further explained the topic.

Similarly, this technique was used at the start of the lecture since teachers asked relevant questions from the students. The students raised their hands and answered the questions according to their understanding. During questioning, students were praised on providing the correct answer. On the other hand, if wrong answers were given, the teacher explained with correction.

Questioning technique was also used at the end of any sub-topic or to relate with the current topic. Few teachers used this as relevant questions were asked from the students one by one to check their understanding of the taught concept. These questions were asked by the students to define. On asking different questions, they described the concepts and then the teachers explained those topics. Through this technique, students were attentive and ready to learn something new. This was for the revision of their previously presented related knowledge and was used by the teachers frequently while teaching any concept, topic or sub-topic. Following field note illustrates this aspect:

> The teacher asked about the "Capacitor". One of the students replied. Then the teacher asked if there was any other student to describe, but no one was ready to explain. The teacher then elaborated the term with detail and presented different examples for a complete understanding of the students. (Field note Phy 3.5)

Another technique used by a few teachers was the use of different examples. These used examples were taken from daily life for a better understanding of the students. During an observation, while teaching the human body skeleton, one of the science teachers provided relevant examples. These examples were used to clarify the topics with an understandable way. Students remained engaged and active during this practice. In a lecture by a participant, the teacher explained about 'Heart Attack' with different examples. The following field note describes one more example regarding this aspect:

> Then the teacher explained about 'Branches of Physics'. One by one, all the branches were discussed after writing these on board. Furthermore, relevant examples were provided as to where these branches might be used? (Field note Phy 3.3)

Summary: Analysis of Classroom Observations

Classroom observations were conducted to explore science teachers' pedagogical practices used for the development of CT skills among secondary school students in a natural setting. Twelve science teachers from 4 schools teaching Physics, Chemistry and Biology were observed while teaching their subjects. Teachers were observed six times while teaching different topics in the classes. All observations lasted for 35 minutes and the purpose of the observations was communicated to both teachers and students. The observations were video recorded by the researcher personally. Filed notes were also prepared for the interpretation of observational data. All observations were analysed based on four themes, that is, classroom atmosphere, teachers' interaction/engagement in the classroom, the focus of the study/explanation of different concepts and pedagogical practices used in the classes. All classrooms were properly ventilated with abundance sunlight coming in through the windows. All teachers used the lecture method to complete their topics in the given 35 minutes. The whiteboard was used in all classrooms during observations. Most of the participants started their lecture by greeting the students, writing the topic on the whiteboard after entering the class. Some of the teachers asked about that day's topic to be taught. In most of the classrooms, there was little interaction among science teachers and students. Most of the time, teachers seemed to remain busy at the whiteboard. Just a few students sitting in front of the teachers interacted during the explanation of the different concepts. The main focus of the teachers was the completion of the lecture with its topics and sub-topics in the provided time. The teachers explained the concepts and topics with different methods like use of a whiteboard, discussion, questionings, description through examples and making diagrams, but there was no special focus on developing CT skills of the students in secondary school science classes.

CHAPTER 5

Findings, Discussion and Recommendations

Introduction and Overview of the Study

In this chapter, findings are summarised and discussed, followed by some recommendations for policy, practice and future research. Findings are obtained from the qualitative content analysis of education policy documents, semi-structured interviews and classroom observations regarding pedagogy for the development of CT skills. The main focus of the data collection methods was to analyse education policy documents and science teachers' practices for developing CT skills among secondary level students. The findings of the study are explained according to research questions that were developed in the light of the literature review and conceptual framework.

The purpose of the current study was to develop an understanding of how the science teachers interpret and enact education policy's recommendations for developing critical thinking skills among secondary school students of public schools in Punjab (Pakistan).

The overall approach for the current study was qualitative with multiple case study design. Purposive sampling technique was used in the selection of education policy documents, that is, National Education Policy (2009), National Curriculum for Physics, Chemistry and Biology for Grades IX-X (2006) and twelve secondary school science teachers teaching the same subjects. Collected data from education policy documents, science teachers' semi-structured interviews and classroom observations were analysed through qualitative content analysis with the facilitation of *Nvivo* 11 software.

Findings of the study revealed different aspects according to the research questions regarding the pedagogy deployed for developing CT skills among secondary school science students. The results were explored based on the analysis of education policy documents, science teachers' perceptions and enacted practices regarding pedagogy for the development of CT skills among secondary school students. The findings of the study can be illustrated through the following figure:

Figure 5.1: Results of analysis of different aspects regarding CT skills development

Findings

The current study aimed to develop an understanding of how science teachers interpret and enact education policy's recommendations for developing critical thinking skills among secondary school students in public schools. The overarching question for this study was: How do science teachers interpret and enact education policy's recommendations for developing critical thinking skills among secondary school students in public schools?

This study is guided by the following sub-questions:

1. What are the recommendations of education policies for the development of CT skills among secondary school students in public schools?

2. What are the science teachers' interpretations of education policy documents' recommendations for the development of CT skills among secondary school students in public schools?

3. What are the science teachers' enactment practices related to education policy documents' recommendations for the development of CT skills among secondary school students in public schools?

4. What are the gaps between education policy documents' recommendations and teachers' enactment practices related to the development of CT skills among secondary school students in public schools?

To address these research questions, data from education policy documents, semi-structured interviews and classroom observations were analysed through qualitative content analysis using *Nvivo* 11 software. The findings are discussed in detail below:

Four Education Policy Documents Recommendations regarding Pedagogy
for the Development of CT Skills

The following four education policy documents were analysed to examine the policy recommendations for the development of CT skills:

- National Education Policy (NEP, 2009);

- National Curriculum for Physics, Grades, IX-X (NCP, 2006);

- National Curriculum for Chemistry, Grades, IX-X (NCC, 2006); and

- National Curriculum for Biology, Grades, IX-X (NCB, 2006).

Qualitative content analysis was used for data analysis through *Nvivo* 11 software. The data was analysed based on four categories, that is, the aim of education/curriculum and Students Learning Outcomes (SLOs), the importance of CT, pedagogical practices for developing CT skills and assessment and CT. These categories were designed to address the objectives and research questions.

The findings related to education policy documents are illustrated through the following figure.

Figure 5.2: *A n a l y s i s   r e s u l t s   o f   e d u c a t i o n   p* ·
regarding pedagogy for developing CT skills

The first aspect was the aim of education and curriculum with students' learning outcomes (SLOs) described in these education policy documents. The analysis of these documents revealed that higher-order skills should be developed in secondary level science students as one of the aims of education is to "Develop a self-reliant individual, capable of analytical and original thinking, a responsible member of society and a global citizen" (NEP, 2009, p. 18) and to make responsible, confident and effective members of the community. The NEP (2009), focuses on developing CT skills for twenty-first-century learners. The Physics curriculum also emphasizes on developing problem-solving skills in secondary school science students with the ability of reasoning, observation, argumentation and evaluation. The Chemistry curriculum aims to produce independent thinkers to solve real-life problems with decision-making skills.

Similarly, the Biology curriculum aims to produce competent individuals having rationale and logic to solve the problems of daily life. The emphasis in curriculum policy documents is given on learning outcomes. For quality education, teachers' quality, pedagogy, curriculum, textbooks and assessment are suggested to be improved.

The second aspect was the importance of CT described in these education policy documents. CT is emphasised due to its importance through different elements. Accordingly, students should have the skills like investigation, asking questions, rationale thinking, identification of problems, creativity, curiosity, experimentation, critical thinking and problem-solving. In NEP (2009), critical thinking is focused on producing independent life-long learners. The Physics curriculum document, emphasises conceptual understanding with problem-solving. The Chemistry curriculum accentuates that students are expected to solve problems with investigation, reasoning and observation to become decision-makers. The Biology curriculum also focuses on CT skills development. Students' learning is suggested with questioning, problem-solving and decision-making strategies. Scientific understanding of living things has been described as the main aim of the Biology curriculum. In all the education policy documents, teachers are expected to become interactive with modern innovative techniques to produce CT in students. Similarly, students are also expected to have abilities of identification, analysis, problem-solving and creativity to solve real-life problems.

The next main aspect suggested was pedagogical practices for developing CT skills described in these education policy documents. The analysis revealed the recommended student-centred pedagogical practices such as questioning, problem-based learning, cooperative learning, problem-solving, group work, debates, discussion, diagrams, flow charts, use of audio-visual aids and activity-based learning. In NEP (2009), student-centred pedagogy has been emphasised for quality education. Focus is on self-directed learning, inquiry, teamwork, problem-solving and critical thinking. The Physics curriculum suggests student-centred and interactive approaches with recommended pedagogical practices like investigation, discussion, problem-solving, students' involvement and laboratory work. Teachers are encouraged to teach the lessons based on questions and activities to make the students creative and critical thinkers. They are suggested to use different pedagogical practices like problem-solving, questioning, cooperative learning, discussion, debates and students' engagement. The Chemistry curriculum also focuses on student-centred pedagogy with interactive, practical, participative, inquiry-based and analytical skills. Recommended pedagogical practices are activity-based and learner-centred approaches like active participation, laboratory work, demonstration, workshops, group work and teaching through diagrams and flow charts. In the Biology curriculum too, the focus is on student-centred, activity and inquiry-based strategies. The recommended pedagogical practices are group work, the team setting, the formulation of questioning with rationale thinking, audio-video presentation, diagrams, graphs, flowcharts, demonstration, investigation, debates and drawing. For teachers, creative and innovative teaching are recommended in all education policy documents. They are encouraged to use student-centred and inquiry-based pedagogy. Furthermore, training is suggested for in-service teachers with pedagogy, pedagogical knowledge, assessment practices, multi-grade teaching and monitoring and evaluation.

The last aspect of the education policy documents' analysis was an assessment of CT skills. In all the education policy documents, different assessment tools are suggested for the implementation in formative and summative assessment. Questions are suggested based on analysis, synthesis and evaluation to assess candidates' problem-solving and higher-order thinking skills through quizzes, worksheets, observations, learning by doing, discussion and diagrams. Furthermore, in the practical examination, the main aim should be to develop problem-solving, daily life and investigation skills of the students. The question paper for the Board of Intermediate and Secondary Education (BISEs) should be based on curriculum as defined by policy rather than textbooks, which is suggested for paper setters. For quality education, analytical thinking is considered utmost important. Rote learning is discouraged on the premise that it hinders the mental growth of the students. The assessment system and its recommended tools focus on CT in both formative and summative assessments. The examination system suggested is based on competency and problem solving, focusing on assessing higher-order thinking. In theory assessment, 40% of questions are recommended to measure higher abilities based on problem solving and application.

Perceptions of Secondary Level Science Teachers regarding Pedagogy for the Development of CT Skills.

Semi-structured interviews were conducted with purposely selected 12 science teachers teaching Physics, Chemistry and Biology. The purpose was to explore their perceptions regarding pedagogy for the development of CT skills. Data were analysed through qualitative content analysis with the facilitation of *Nvivo* 11 software. Findings were divided into six sub-themes, that is, perception about the concept of CT, the importance of CT, the focus of the department on training/ professional development of the teachers, pedagogical practices used by teachers in the classroom, assessment system regarding CT and barriers in developing CT skills.

| Perceptions about CT | •Conceptual study, students' ability of understanding, deep thinking, to discourage rote learning, and thinking with reasoning. |

| Importance of CT | •For twenty-first century skill
•For quality education
•Competency building
•Usage in practical life
•For decision making in preparation for the future |

| Focus of the Department/ Training of the Teachers | •No focus of the Education Department for CT skills development.
•No refresher or professional development course or trainings for CT skills development.
•No inspection and motivation by the department or higher authorities.
•Focus on passing examination and other activities like cleanliness, enrollment etc. |

| Ppedagogical Practices used | •Pedagogical practice used to get good marks.
•Group work, questioning, practical-based methods, use of whiteboard, charts, diagrams, and models.
•Downloaded video clips and models of animals for demonstration |

| Assessment and CT | •Dissatisfied with the current assessment system.
•Suggested assessment criteria for implementation for CT skills in BISE papers.
•Questions demanding CT were suggested to be included.
•Suggested to revisit and revise the whole assessment system. |

| Barrieres | •Department, teachers, and current assessment system has no focus on CT skills development.
•Need of implication the pedagogy and assessment system.
•Trainings and refresher courses for CT skills development were suggested.
•Limited practical experimentation apparatus.
•The top-down change was required by the participants for CT skills development. |

Figure 5.3:   A n a l y s i s   a n d   r e s u l t s   o f   t e a c h e r s'
developing CT skills

The first aspect was science teachers' perceptions of the concept of CT.

Teachers described this concept in different terms like conceptual study, students' ability of understanding, deep thinking, discouraging rote learning and thinking with reasoning.

The next aspect was participants' perceptions about the importance of CT, especially in science subjects at the secondary level. All the teachers agreed upon its importance for all science subjects. Most of the teachers were of the view that in the twenty-first century, the purpose of education should be the development of reasoning skills in students. It was admitted that quality education might be achieved through conceptual study and complete understanding, which were considered necessary for the development of CT skills in secondary level science students being the age of decision making. Few of the participants admitted its importance because of its role in logical, rationale and conceptual based study habits. One more aspect regarding the importance of CT described by the few participants considered it as competency building among the secondary level science students.

In the same way, CT was perceived important for science students because of its usage in practical life and practical work in science subjects, which was considered necessary in upcoming academic and practical lives of the students. CT skills development was perceived most useful at this stage for decision-making in going for medical, engineering or other fields. In the same way, few of the participants considered it important due to the preparation of future students regarding the different fields of education, innovation and further progress in their practical lives.

Focus/encouragement by the department for the development of CT skills was the next aspect. According to all participants' perspective, there was no focus on the department for CT skills development. Similarly, no refresher or professional development course or training was conducted regarding this aspect. All participants were of the view that there was no inspection and motivation by the department or higher authorities for this specific aspect. The focused elements by monitoring and inspection officers were only attendance, cleanliness, enrolment and Learning and Numeracy Drive (LND). LND was monitored by Monitoring and Evaluation Assistants (MEAs) for grade 3. The focus of the department and higher authorities was only on passing the examination and getting good marks. Newly recruited participants had just received two weeks of subject-specific induction training without focus of CT skills development in their teaching practices.

The next important aspect was teachers' perceptions about pedagogical practices for the development of CT skills since this was the main objective of the study. According to the participants' perceptions, they used different pedagogical practice in their science classrooms, focusing only to get students' good marks or pass the maximum students instead of developing CT skills. According to a few of the participants' perceptions, group work method was used because of the large size of class instead of cooperative learning, since they were unaware of this specific method. Similarly, most of the participants used the questioning technique to make the students attentive. One of the teachers used it in quiz competitions. The discussion method was also used with the questioning technique by a few participants. Some of the participants used a practical-based method like learning by doing for students' better understanding since they perceived that practical and activity-based teaching methods were useful for teaching science students. Most of the teachers stated that they used whiteboard, charts, diagrams and models as audio-visual aids. One of the participants narrated about the use of downloaded video clips and living organs of animals for demonstration and students' understanding in his classrooms. The science teachers used these pedagogical practices in their daily teaching of science subject but not with the focus on CT skills development.

The next aspect was the assessment system and CT. Teachers were not satisfied with the current assessment system for the development of CT skills, since it was not promoting CT in science students. They perceived that through rote learning, students might get maximum marks in different subjects. Therefore, teachers and students, both emphasised getting good marks. All participants demanded top-down change in the assessment system for secondary schools. They suggested questions requiring CT to be included since in the present assessment system; most of the questions were based on rote-learning and repetition. Therefore, students got maximum marks without focusing on CT skills development. For paper setters, higher-order thinking and creativity type questions were suggested to be included in the annual question papers. Few of the participants suggested to include a maximum of how and why type questions in the question papers.

The final aspect was about facing barriers regarding the developing CT skills by science teachers. According to most of the participants, department, teachers and current assessment system had no focus on CT skills development. There was no suggestion of any technique or assessment system for the promotion of CT. Training and refresher courses were suggested for teachers' professional development with no focus on CT skills development. The department also focused on getting good results and marks of the students; therefore, the teachers' emphasis was on developing students' abilities to get good marks. Furthermore, limited practical experimentation apparatus was reported, due to which students were unable to do all practical work in laboratories to practice their theoretical concepts.

Teachers' Practices for Developing CT S

Twelve science teachers teaching Physics, Chemistry or Biology from four schools were observed six times while teaching their science subjects in natural settings. All observations were analysed based on four themes, that is, the classroom atmosphere, teachers' interaction/engagement in the classroom, focus of the study/ explanation of different concepts and pedagogical practices used in the classes. The following figure illustrates the findings:

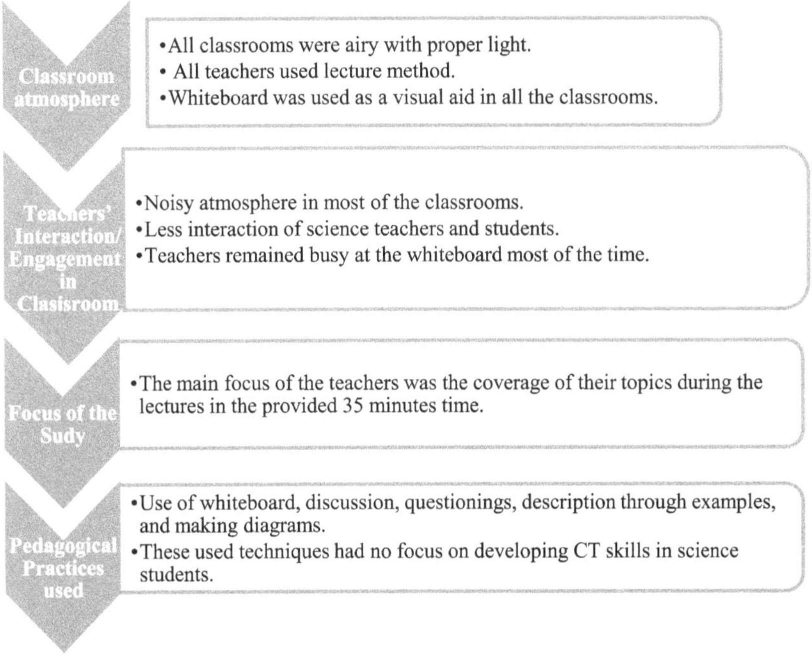

Figure 5.4: A n a l y s i s o f r e s u l t s o f t h e t e a c h e
developing CT skills

All classrooms were airy with proper light. All teachers used the lecture method to teach the topic in provided 35 minutes. The whiteboard was used in all the classrooms. In most of the classes, the noisy atmosphere was observed. That is why there was less interaction between science teachers and students. Most of the time, teachers seemed to remain busy at the whiteboard while explaining different concepts and questions. Doing this, students sitting at the back were observed passively due to the lecture method and no interaction of the teacher with the students. Just a few students sitting in front of the teachers showed interest by interacting with the teachers through the explanation of different topics and subtopics. The main focus of the teachers was the completion of their topic during the lectures in the provided 35 minutes. Few of the classrooms were observed with a pleasant learning environment. Students were engaged through different techniques like the use of a whiteboard, discussion, questionings, description through examples and making diagrams according to the situation of the lecture, but the methods used had no focus on developing CT skills in science students.

Discussion of the Results

The objectives of the study were to analyse education policy documents (National Education Policy, 2009 and National Curriculum for Physics, Chemistry and Biology for Grades IX-X, 2006) for developing CT skills, to explore teachers' perceptions and enacted practices regarding the development of CT skills. Education policy documents were analysed through qualitative content analysis. Teachers' perceptions about CT skills development were explored through semi-structured interviews and finally, the teachers were observed in their classrooms with video recordings and reflective field notes to explore teachers' practices for the development of CT skills. The following is a detailed explanation in view of the research questions:

Analysis of Research Question 1: Education Policy Documents Analysis

This section is about the first sub-question: (1) What are the recommendations expressed in education policies for the development of CT skills among secondary school students in public schools?

To address this research question, four purposely selected education policy documents were analysed to develop an understanding regarding the recommended pedagogy for the development of CT skills in secondary school students. These documents were National Education Policy (2009) and National Curriculum for

Physics, Chemistry and Biology (2006) for Grades IX-X.

The analysis revealed that in the education policy documents, the aim of

education had been described to develop critical and higher-order thinking skills to

make the students independent and responsible member of society. NEP (2009)

describes the aim of education to make the students self-reliant and independent with

the rationale that thinking is necessary to become a responsible member and global

citizen. The curriculum of Physics also focuses on problem-solving and other life

skills through observation, reasoning and argumentation. In the same way, the

curricula for Chemistry and Biology also aim to develop independent thinkers to

solve their problems with decision-making skills. In the curriculum of Chemistry, the

aim has been described as "To produce students who will be capable of doing

independent thinking, asking questions and looking for answers on their own" (NCC,

2006, p. 1). In students' learning outcomes, CT of the students is identified. Teacher

quality, curriculum, pedagogy and assessment are emphasised to reach the goal of

quality education. All education policy documents emphasise on the importance of

CT. Teachers are expected to become interactive in their lessons with questioning and

other activity-based techniques. Students are also expected to have the ability to

identify, analyse and solve their problems. In the curriculum document of Chemistry

(2006), it has been described as "Teachers are encouraged to design their lessons in

such a way that suitable questions and activities are incorporated to develop various

types and levels of thinking in students, including analysis, evaluation, critical

thinking and creative thinking" (NCC, 2006, p. 28). For science teachers, training is

suggested for conceptual understanding, problem-solving and practical work to

enhance their practices in pedagogical content knowledge, subject matter, assessment, monitoring and evaluation. In curriculum development, CT skills are focused on reflecting important social issues, promote self-directed learning, problem-solving, inquiry-based teaching and teamwork. Regarding developing CT skills among students, the assessment system is discussed in the NEP (2009) to achieve quality education. The practice of rote learning is discouraged; rather, the focus is on critical and analytical thinking skills to produce independent and life-long learners. In the view of National Education Policy (2009), the suggested pedagogical practices for the development of CT skills are questioning, inquiry-based, problem-solving, cooperative learning, discussion, active involvement, conversation and learning-by-doing. In the curriculum documents, recommended learner-centred pedagogical practices are inquiry-based learning, group work, workshops, diagrams, flow charts, graphs and activity-based approaches like laboratory work, fieldwork and demonstration. Biology curriculum describes that there should "Be student-centred, assisting students in deriving their concepts from evidence and providing practical opportunities to develop individual reasoning abilities and motor skills" (NCB, 2006, p. 90). CT skills development has also been focused on assessment system in education policy documents. Analysis, synthesis and evaluation based questions are suggested to be given a maximum place in the question paper. Furthermore, questions regarding understanding, argument, explanation and reasoning for the development of higher-order thinking are recommended as described in the policy. In the Chemistry curriculum, it has been described as "Assessment should measure the capacity of students for critical judgment" (NCC, 2006, p. 48). In the same documents, all cognitive skills as knowledge, comprehension, analysis, application, synthesis and evaluations are suggested to be measured through reasoning. In the Chemistry curriculum, it is recommended that the assessment questions should be based on different stages of Bloom's Taxonomy. Higher abilities should be given 40% weightage in the assessment. The question paper should be based on curriculum rather than the textbook as well, as these should be based on higher-order and problem-solving skills. Students must be able to analyse data from the investigation. The results were found in the study conducted by Arif (2011) to analyse the Mathematics curriculum at secondary school level in Pakistan with the analysis of no achievement of four objectives as application of concepts in Math, enhancing ability of the reasoning among students, analytical and critical examination of the students and spirit of discovery and exploration. The focus was on logical reasoning and activity-based learning. Another study conducted in 2004 (Rehman, 2004) with reference to the Chemistry curriculum. The study analysed that the curriculum was not designed according to the needs of the modern age.

Analysis of Research Question 2: Teacher CT Skills Development

The second research question was: What are the science teachers' interpretations of education policy documents' recommendations for the development of CT skills among secondary school students in public schools?

This research question was explored through science teachers' semi-structured interviews for their perception of pedagogy for the development of CT skills in science students.

All the participants were aware of the concept of critical thinking as they defined it in different terms like conceptual study, the ability of students for understanding, knowledge with deep thinking, reasoning behind knowledge and to discourage rote learning. One of the participants explained it as the development of deep thinking in science students with logic and rationale. All the participants admitted its importance especially in science subjects at the secondary level regarding different factors like the purpose of education, need for science subjects, decision making, to face challenges and make progress in every walk of life in science subjects at the secondary level. One of the Chemistry teachers explained that the purpose of education could not be fulfilled without developing CT skills in science subjects. Logic and rationale were needed for the students in teaching and learning to answer the questions with reasoning and logic. Furthermore, it was narrated that education should produce critical thinkers. In science subjects, it was focused due to its importance in different activities and practical experiments with a conceptual understanding based on observations and discussion for the decision-making process.

According to all the participants, there was no focus or encouragement by the department for the development of CT skills in secondary level science students. No refresher courses and professional development training were conducted regarding this. Few of the participants explained about the training by Directorate of Staff Development (DSD) renamed as Quaid-e-Azam Academy for Educational Development (QAED), but these workshops were subject-specific. Most of the participants were of the view that they used different pedagogical practices like group work, discussion, questioning, activity-based, practical-based, experimental, learning by doing and whiteboard, charts and models as audio-visual aids. But the focus of these classroom techniques was not developing CT skills among secondary level science students. Some of the participants used group work instead of co-operative learning. Different previous researchers have used this method (Huang et al., 2017; Nezami et al., 2013). One of the Physics teachers explained about pedagogy in such a way:

> I make different groups of students to get them to understand the specific
> phenomenon. There are students of different calibre. Through group work, they

can learn in a better way. The weak students also may learn well from intelligent students. Thus, this strategy is useful for science students. (Physics Teacher-2).

Teachers reported that they were using the questioning technique in teaching science. This technique is used for CT skills development as reported in some previous studies (Inamullah et al., 2016; Rashid & Qaisar, 2016; Santoso et al., 2018). One of the participants described the use of a discussion technique since this has been used with questioning by previous researchers (Bevan, 2017; Khan, 2017). The following field note describes the discussion technique used by one of the participants:

> Discussion is an important technique, but seldom used in my classroom. If there are some topics which need to be explained, they are required to be discussed. In this way, students have positive and negative aspects of the concept. So, they may understand it. (Physics Teacher-3)

Some of the teachers also used practical-based work as one teacher admitted it compulsory for the understanding of the conceptual study. Because of the limited apparatus, there were no practical experiments. Teachers were of the view that through practical work and learning by doing, students can get conceptual study. Audio-visual aids like whiteboards, charts and models were also being used to a certain extent by few teachers as one of the participants explained that he usually showed charts and models related to any topic as an introduction to students in the laboratory. Practical work was used in the previous study by Alosaimi (2013) with discussion and questioning. One of the participants explained that because of the shortage of the practical apparatus, the use of audio-visual aids was limited. This was done with charts and models too.

Furthermore, participants were not satisfied with the current assessment system since they perceived that the current assessment system was not promoting CT skills development among secondary level science students. With the assessment system, students might get good marks through rote-learning and repetition of the questions. Question papers were suggested with a focus on thinking and answering the questions according to students' thinking. It was suggested that conceptual and skilled based questions should be included for assessment to develop CT skills among the students. Furthermore, it was also explored that teachers and students just emphasised on getting good marks by memorising the topics and questions.

One of the participants demanded change from top-down strategy. Education department and officers should focus on implementing the policy action for the development of CT skills. Teachers and students should be ready to accept the change. The system does not focus on students' CT, creativity and expectations to write the answers in their own words. Overall assessment system was suggested to be revised and revisited for the development of CT skills in the question papers taken by BISEs; these should be revisited to include different higher-order thinking questions in the question papers. It was also suggested to revise and revisit the education policy for the CT skills development promotion. Question papers were suggested to be designed, keeping in view CT skills questions that assess secondary level science students of such skills.

The above results show that the main focus of the teachers was to cover the content and pass the students with good marks. They were not focusing on developing CT skills; rather their main aim was to get good grades and pass the students in a board examination. There are similar results from a qualitative study conducted by Alazzi (2008), with 12 secondary school teachers of social studies regarding the perceptions about the teaching of CT in their classrooms. The findings revealed that teachers had limited knowledge about CT, and had not been focused while teaching. In the view of Rehman (2004), activity and demonstrative methods were to be used for teaching Chemistry. Audio-visual aids were suggested to be provided in the classrooms. Examination system should also be based on the objectives of the curriculum, scientific skills, evaluation and attitude instead of just rote learning.

A n a l y s i s   o f   r e s e a r c h   q u e s t i o n   3 :   T e a c h e r

The third research question was: What science teachers' enactment practices are related to education policy documents' recommendations for the development of CT skills among secondary school students in public schools?

To answer this research question, classroom observations were conducted to observe the participants while teaching their respective science subjects, that is, Physics, Chemistry or Biology for 6 lessons. The main focus of these classroom observations was to identify the science teachers' pedagogical practices for the development of CT skills in secondary school students. Analysis of video recordings and field notes revealed that almost all classrooms were ventilated with natural light. All teachers used lecture methods in their classrooms. Most of the participants announced the topics and wrote it on the white-board after entering the class. The main focus of all the participants was the completion of the content in 35 minutes. Less interaction and engagement was found in most of the classrooms since science teachers remained busy writing on the white-board to explain different topics and sub-topics. In doing so, only a few students, usually sitting in front of the teachers, were attentive. This aspect is described in the following field note:

> The students sitting in front of the class were attentive. There was some whispering from the backbenchers. Most of the students were making noise since the teacher was busy writing on the whiteboard. (Field note Phy 1.4)

In a few classrooms, teachers' interactions were observed with in a pleasant classroom atmosphere. Students seemed active and engaged in these classrooms. Such type of observed classes was incorporated with student-centred techniques like questioning, discussion, explanation through examples and the use of charts, models and diagrams.

The questioning technique was used in a few lectures by the participants. This technique was used at different stages of the lecture: at the start for students' brainstorming, in middle or when any sub-topic was completed and at the end to review all lesson. There are similar results to previous studies as questioning for developing CT skills (Inamullah et al., 2016; Rashid & Qaisar, 2016; Santoso et al., 2018). The following field note illustrates the questioning technique by one participant:

> Then the teacher asked, "First of all, tell me about the Chemical Bond". Then some students raised their hands to answer the question. The teacher asked them to describe the definition. The students described the definition one by one. The teacher praised on right answers. (Field note Chem 4.3)

In the same way, few of the teachers used different examples while teaching, as explained in the following field note:

> The teacher explained "Ultrasound Wave", then described its usage with various examples. The first example was given to break a clot of blood. Next was delivered as in bakery items like milk through ultrasonic wave and it is made safe and drinkable for an extended period. In planes and heavy machinery, these are used to diagnose any cracks which are unidentifiable with the human eye. In the same way sea depth is also measured with these waves. (Field note Phy 2.4)

The above findings of education policy documents emphasise different pedagogical practices for the development of CT skills. Teachers also used these to some extent, but not for the development of CT skills, which was true in all classrooms. National and international literature support different pedagogical practices on several academic factors.

Different pedagogical practices support the findings of the study, such as active learning methods, promote CT skills (Azizmalayeri et al., 2012; Kim et al., 2013; Youngblood & Beitz, 2001). Reflective thinking skills proved to be effective in distance teacher education programs (Ali & Buzdar, 2013), investigation and discovery enhanced ability to acquire information and knowledge (Hwang & Chang, 2011), problem-solving and CT skills with discussion, cognitive abilities and cooperative learning (Tseng, Tuan, & Chin, 2013) and close association between CT skills and teachers' professional development (Mahmood, 2017).

Questioning and inquiry-based teaching have been recommended by education policy documents. Also, many previous studies support this technique. An experimental study was conducted by Santoso et al. (2018) to find out the role of questioning in developing critical thinking in learning Chemistry. The experimental design was used with 94 students at the university level. The analysis showed an essential role of questioning in CT skills development. In the same way, the role of teachers' questioning was found useful on students' CT in EFL classroom by Yuliawati, Mahmud, and Muliati (2016). The qualitative descriptive method was used with interviews, field notes and classroom observations. Higher-order thinking questions improved students' CT skills, which were recommended. In another study by Rashid and Qaisar (2016), the focus was the effectiveness of questioning on CT skills development. Through the case study experimental design, questionnaire, observation and field notes were used as data collection methods. Findings of the study revealed the use of questioning in CT skills development. Furthermore, comprising other inquiry based learning on students' CT skills development for science and technology at secondary level , questioning was a more effective methods in teaching 9th-grade Physics students than the lecture method (Hussain, 2011). Socratic questioning to enhance CT skills of the students at university level (Yang, Newby, & Bill, 2005), asking questions for the development of students' CT skills (Bailey & Mentz, 2015) and identification of most effective technique for the achievement and improvement to discover information and CT skills (Blanchard et al., 2010).

The cooperative learning method is also suggested by education policy documents and was used by teachers as group work. Literature also suggests the effectiveness of cooperative learning in academic achievement (Gillies et al., 2008), the effect of cooperative learning on CT of the students at secondary level (Nezami et al., 2013) and the effect of cooperative learning and concept mapping was examined by (Huang et al., 2017) to teach CT skills.

Debates are also suggested to be effective in the development of CT skills at the secondary level (Othman et al., 2015), since this has been an effective teaching method for developing confidence, communication and CT skills (Hall, 2011). The problem-solving technique was also demonstrated to enhance CT, understanding and knowledge acquisition of the students (Kumar & Natarajan, 2007; Snyder & Snyder, 2008).

The above studies showed that different pedagogical practices could promote CT skills development, but in the Pakistani context, teachers fail to focus on developing CT skills among secondary school students since their main emphasis is only for their students to get good grades and marks in BISE exams; however, previous literature has identified practices that is in support these pedagogical practices for developing CT skills.

Analysis of Research Question 4: Gaps between Policy and Practice

The fourth research question of the study was: What are the gaps between education policy documents' recommendations and teachers' enactment practices related to the development of CT skills among secondary school students in public schools?

According to the education policy documents' analysis, different pedagogical practices have been suggested to be used for the development of CT skills. The discussion above shows the gap between policy and practices. Teachers are aware of the concept of CT skills and its importance as they use different pedagogical practices in their classrooms too, but their main focus is to get good grades and marks of the students in the annual examination rather than to develop CT skills. Therefore, the analysis revealed gaps in curriculum policy documents and practices of secondary level science teachers regarding the development of CT skills among students. There is a difference between policy and practice. Education policy documents focus on the importance of CT as an essential skill of the twenty-first century, but in teachers' practices, they have not been enacted.

Education and monitoring officers from the department focus on cleanliness, enrolment, attendance and excellent results. The concept of the result is the pass percentage of greater number of students. They emphasise on getting students passed because of the requirement of the department. A top-down change is needed for the acceptance and implementation of CT skills development. The department and monitoring officers should focus on CT skills development. From the department, there should be appreciation and motivation regarding this. As a teacher described the inspection of the school and its focus in the following words:

> The educational officers, mainly focus on cleanliness, enrolment, Learning and Numeracy Drive (LND) tests of 3rd grade and presence of staff in school, but not on the quality of education. There is no focus or special interest in developing CT skills among students. The monitoring system is just about different activities instead of developing CT skills. (Chemistry Teacher-1)

The refresher courses and induction training should be focused on special instructions regarding the students' development of CT skills. The induction training conducted by the department should have the responsibility to focus on a specific aspect. Even the master trainers who are trained from the QAED should deliver further training, keeping in view the importance of CT. All science teachers used group work, discussion, questioning, activity-based, practical-based, experimental, learning by doing and the use of audio-visual aids techniques in the classroom, but the focus of these classroom techniques was not developing CT skills among secondary level science students. The focus should be only on the development of CT skills and relevant pedagogical practices should be used according to the topic. This is possible with only top-down change and priority of the department.

Assessment is also an essential factor which can play a significant role in developing CT skills. It should be changed according to suggested curriculum documents since it is not promoting CT skills development among secondary level science students. There should be a revision of the assessment system focusing on the development of CT skills. Through the current assessment system, students can get maximum marks through rote learning. The assessment of today is a number game as the students can achieve more than 95% marks in science subjects because deep thinking questions are missing. Paper setters should design the question papers in line with the guidelines of education policy documents. The question papers should be based on conceptual and reasoning basis consistent with the allotted criteria of higher-order thinking in policy documents. How and why type of questions should be used based on curriculum, not on textbooks, so that students may demonstrate their ability to understand the original concept.

From the above discussion, it is clear that top-down change is needed for implementation and revising the assessment system focusing on CT skills development.

Implications for Policy, Practice and Future Research

Implications for Policy

Education policy documents have focused on different aspects concerning CT. One of the objectives was to explore the education policy in documents relating to pedagogy for developing CT skills in secondary level science students. All curriculum policy documents were analysed based on four themes, that is, the aim of education/curriculum & SLOs, the importance of CT, pedagogical practices for developing CT skills and assessment system for CT. In all aspects, CT skills have been emphasised. Being a twenty-first-century skill, it has been described as an important aspect of acquiring education. The aim of education has been to produce individuals having the capacity of logical, analytical, conceptual reasoning and confidence with problem-solving, independent thinking, rational thinking and with an effective contribution to the society since the NEP (2009) aims to "Develop a self-reliant individual, capable of analytical and original thinking, a responsible member of society and a global citizen" (NEP, 2009, p. 19). In the same way, the Physics curriculum also explains CT as "Develop the ability to describe and explain concepts, principles, systems, processes and applications related to Physics and develop the thinking process, imagination, ability to solve problems, data management, investigating and communication skills" (NCP, 2006, p. 5). CT has been defined to produce independent and rationale thinkers to make real-life decisions in their personal, social and professional life. Furthermore, it has been illustrated to "Enable all students to develop their capacities as successful learners, confident individuals, responsible citizens and effective contributors to society to solve everyday life problems, logical in oral and writing" (NCB, 2006, p. 1).

The importance of CT has been explained for problem-solving and decision-making process. Pedagogical practices for developing CT skills suggested in these documents are student-centred, activity-based learning, questioning, discussion, cooperative learning, flowchart, graphs, flow chart, group work, demonstration, investigation and debates. NEP (2009) suggests that student-centred methods of teaching develop the capacity for self-directed learning, the spirit of inquiry, critical thinking, problem-solving and team-work for the students. Accordingly, questioning, problem-solving, discussion, cooperative learning, debates and students' involvement are also suggested. NCC (2006) also suggests student-centred, activity-based, interactive, participative practical, laboratory work, workshop, group work, inquiry-based, diagrams, flowcharts, graphs, fieldwork and inquiry-based approaches. In NCB (2006), group work, team setting, formulation of questions, audio-video presentation, diagrams, graphs, flowcharts, demonstration, investigation, debates and drawing are listed as potential pedagogical practices.

The assessment system is also suggested for developing CT skills based on analysis, synthesis and evaluation, focusing on developing higher-order thinking skills. According to NEP (2009), assessment should be focused on the development of analytical and critical thinking. Different assessment tools are suggested to be practised instead of those traditionally used in both formative and summative assessments. NCP (2006), suggests analysis, synthesis and evaluation based questions should be given maximum place to assess candidates' problem-solving and higher-order thinking skills. According to NCC (2006), assessments should measure the capacity of students for critical judgment. Practical examinations should be conducted to explore problem solving, daily life experiences and investigation skills of the students. NCB (2006) focuses on assessment and evaluation based on problem-solving and competency with different assessment devices like worksheets, quizzes, observation, diagram completion, discussions, learning by doing and review questions. The focus of examination should be on curriculum-based instead of the textbook.

The above discussion illustrates that all of the education policy documents focus on developing CT skills, regarding its importance, and alternative suggested pedagogical practices for the development of CT skills and diverse assessment techniques of assessment focusing development of CT skills. According to the teachers' perspectives and realising the importance of CT in mind, they are unable to implement the recommended pedagogical practices for developing CT skills. Each document has three main aspects: that is, the aim of education, pedagogy and assessment system and CT has been emphasised repeatedly. There is a need for implementation of these. Teachers should be provided with curriculum policy documents for their understanding, describing the aim of education and the importance of CT skills. The curriculum experts should keep in mind what is needed for ground-realities for the implementation of CT. Teachers should be given specific training or refresher courses in view of the guidelines provided by these policy documents. The education officers should also focus on this phenomenon. There is needed a top down change approach for implementation.

Similarly, paper setters should concentrate on designing question papers based on logical and analytical thinking. There is a need for implication of the policy and should be revisited according to the needs of the teachers, students and different other stakeholders. The current policy documents emphasise various aspects of quality education, teachers' pedagogical practices and assessment system, which should be consistent with the ground realities. After the top-down change, through implementation into practice critical thinkers might be produced.

Implications for Practice

There is a need to develop science teachers' awareness of the education policy documents, especially related to their purpose, pedagogy and assessment system. Findings suggest that teachers are not provided with copies of the policy documents; therefore, it is needed to share the policy documents so teachers are aware of their specific content.

All education policy documents recognize the different aspect of CT skills development, which should be focused on the aim of education. In each curriculum policy document, there is great emphasis on developing CT skills. Teachers are aware of this concept, but in different terms. There is a lot of evidence from literature regarding the importance of CT skills as it has been considered the twenty-first-century skill and essential for demographic, informational, economic and technological growth (Bialik & Fadel, 2015). In the context of education, it has vital importance since it has been proved essential for the progress and development of students as well as the whole education system (Spatariu et al., 2016). For the twenty-first century learners, CT has become an essential skill and the learning of CT skills is essential to become effective reflective thinker (Higgins, 2015).

Therefore, teachers should try to cultivate CT skills among students. In schools and classrooms, students should be presented with real-life situations to participate in learning activities (Gutek, 2013). The analysis of observational data revealed that there was no focus on practical experimentation by science teachers. Through activities and practical experimentation, literature supports CT skills development which has been recommended by the education policy documents too.

Doing this may be fruitful for them in solving problems of real-life to become a productive citizen of the country.

Science teachers might make the students do the recommended practical experiments, producing an ability in them to solve the problems through observation, analysis and evaluation. The education department might focus and monitor practical experimentation requirement to ensure that students change in critical thinking through learning by doing, problem-solving and hands-on activities (Schiro, 2012). According to the teachers' point of view, there is no focus on the department and educational officers on the development of CT skills. They have not received any specific training or professional development course in learning how to implement CT skills. In this regard, teachers might be provided with education policy documents, so they may be aware of the recommendations of the education policy documents. The department might focus on this. Professional development sessions might be conducted for the science teachers to enhance their knowledge, skills and attitude towards the development of CT skills since professional development sessions have been demonstrated to be useful for the promotion of CT skills (Bailey & Mentz, 2015).

The findings of the current study revealed that the teacher-participants often used the lecture method in their classrooms. Less interaction was observed in the classes while teachers were busy writing on their white-boards. Students, sitting in front of the teacher, seemed engaged while, the seated at the back were passive. To enthuse students, teachers might engage the students through different interactive activities according to the topic since active learning has a positive effect on the enhancement of students' CT skills (Kim et al., 2013). Through the engagement of different learning activities and problem-solving, students learn CT skills. A few teachers explained that they could not use specific methods due to over-populated classrooms. In such condition, cooperative learning might be used since it has been used for CT skills development in other various contexts (Huang et al., 2017; Nezami et al., 2013; Ting & Abdullah, 2020). The education policy documents have recommended different pedagogical practices for developing CT skills, as described in the data analysis section. The participants used some of the pedagogical practices, but the main emphasis was on just telling the content during class time. The used pedagogical practices were questioning, discussion, group work, explanation through examples and practical work.

During the classroom observations, some of the teachers used the questioning technique. This practice was used at different times and intervals of the lesson, at the start of the lesson for brain-storming, in the middle of the lecture for revision of taught content and at the end of the session to clarify the topic through questioning and seeking responses from the students. As discussed earlier, the aim of these pedagogical practices used by the science teachers was not CT skills development but to complete the content and pass the students in BISE examinations. In the Pakistani context, Rashid and Qaisar (2016) conducted research which showed that the questioning strategy was effective for CT skills development in 4th-grade students. Similarly, the role of questioning has also been shown to be significant in a study by Inamullah et al. (2016). He found multi-type questioning with higher-order thinking promoted CT in the students. Furthermore, a positive and significant relationship was found between questioning with CT. This experimental study proved that questioning has an important role in CT skills development with inference, prediction and analysis (Santoso et al., 2018). Since these relevant studies demonstrated helpfulness through the questioning techniques in improving CT skills among students, the science teachers should use this technique for specific purposes according to the nature of the topic.

Few of the participants used the discussion method with questioning. This method also has significance due to its contribution to CT skills development. Through this method of teaching, there is confidence building in students since discussion fosters logic, reason and rationale. The participants of the current study used this technique to explain the concept in further detail. Questioning and discussion have proved fruitful for developing CT skills (Bevan, 2017; Khan, 2017).

A few of the participants used charts, models and practical experiments in their classrooms. The participants used these practices without the focus of CT skills development. The literature has also suggested these pedagogical practices aided CT skills development. Active learning methods with group-based learning, engagement of learning activities to solve science problems were used also in the study (Azizmalayeri et al., 2012; Kim et al., 2013). These pedagogical practices should be used for the development of CT skills to make learners into logical and independent thinkers.

The science teachers might also use inquiry based-teaching learning methods for the development of CT. This method has also been proved significant to promote CT skills in students since according to the results of a study; inquiry-based practice with arguments, deduction and evaluation information gained and the process of critical thinking was proved to be effective in CT skills development among the students (Agustini & Suyatna, 2018; Phonna et al., 2021). Similarly, one more experimental study by Duran and Dökme (2016) found the positive effect of inquiry-based learning on students' CT skills in science and technology course from a post-test designed experimental group. Therefore, science teachers should use this technique too for the promotion of CT skills in science subjects.

Debates, dialogues and practical work, have also been used in the past for the development of CT skills as the education policy documents recommend, but the teachers' perceptions and enacted practices had not revealed these practices to occur. These practices should be embedded into teaching science subjects for CT skills development: an experimental study has shown to be a useful technique in CT skills enhancement (Othman et al., 2015). In the same way, another study used problem-solving examples and monitoring with dialogue for the development of CT skills (Abrami et al., 2015). The science teachers enact these specific techniques during their relevant lectures to promote CT in science students.

The findings explain that teachers had no knowledge of and no training was offered by the department regarding CT skills development, although the focus of the department, may be to conduct professional development sessions for the science teachers to improve their pedagogical practices. According to a previous study by Bailey and Mentz (2015), teachers' pedagogical skills for the development of CT skills were improved through professional development sessions of the teachers. Therefore, the training institutions such as QAED might conduct such type of sessions for CT skills development.

In the education policy documents, the emphasis is on the assessment system with the inclusion of questions, based on higher-order thinking skills. In the subjective part, paper setters are suggested to design the paper with a suggested weight of the questions requiring CT (NCB, 2006; NCP, 2006). Nevertheless, in the question papers, these types of questions are rare and the students do not respond to these, but rather answer rote responses. Most of the previous questions are repeated in exams. Teachers use guess papers or past year papers to get the students prepared for the examination. In this way, because of no emphasis of the department, CT skill is not taken seriously by the teachers. Therefore, the assessment system might be revisited to include how and why type questions. Students then have to think and answer with reason. Through changes in the assessment system, students and teachers might begin to focus on CT skills development to further improve this important skill. There is a need for reform of the assessment system as well as recommendations of the education policy document.

One more finding of the study was the focus on getting good grades and marks. The department, teachers and students want to pass the examination. The assessment system recommends questions demanding higher-order thinking and the education policy documents focus on the assessment of curriculum-based, not on rote text-book recalls. Hence, the assessment system needs to be revised. Paper setters should focus on recommended suggestions and a section might be specified for higher-order thinking skills. All stakeholders like education authorities, policymakers, educational managers, headteachers, teachers, students and paper setters might implement CT skills keeping in view its importance.

Overall, there is a need for the implication of the policy to practice. Thus, according to the recommended pedagogical practices, the department and teachers might focus on students' CT skills development. A top-down change is needed with the cooperation and facilitation of all stakeholders to make the twenty-first-century learners critical and logical thinkers.

Implications for Future Research

The current study focused on two aspects of education in Pakistan: policy documents' analysis specifically the call for the development of critical thinking skills and science teachers' perspectives on the teaching of CT skills. Further studies might be conducted to find out the effect of any one strategy or combined strategies to develop CT skills in the science students. Previous studies with different pedagogies for the enhancement in CT skills like developing CT through questioning (Inamullah et al., 2016; Khorraminejad et al., 2020; Rashid & Qaisar, 2016; Santoso et al., 2018). Similarly, cooperative learning has also been used for the development of CT skills (Huang et al., 2017; Nezami et al., 2013; Ting & Abdullah, 2020). Questioning and discussions have proved to be effective techniques for the development of CT (Bevan, 2017; Khan, 2017). Inquiry-based practices and learning were also shown to be effective for CT skills development (Agustini & Suyatna, 2018; Duran & Dökme, 2016). Debates and dialogues have also been used as teaching methods for the enhancement of CT (Abrami et al., 2015; Othman et al., 2015). Although these various pedagogic strategies have enhanced the learning of CT skills, they have not been incorporated into normal classroom practice.

The current study focused on students for CT skills development in the education policy document and curriculum documents of science subjects (Physics, Chemistry and Biology). Future studies may be conducted with other school subjects such as Mathematics, Urdu, English, Pakistan Studies, Islamic Studies and other subjects. These subjects may be analysed with respect to CT skills development. For example, in the English curriculum, the aim has been stated as to apply CT for interaction with text and in SLOs section, it has been described as follows:

> Such activities are to be incorporated at each grade that caters for progressive cognitive development from lower-level intellectual skills of simple knowledge and comprehension to higher-order skills of analysis, synthesis and evaluation so as to nurture the ability of reasoning, problem-solving, critical thinking and creativity. (NCE, 2006, p. 3)

Similarly, the national curriculum for Pakistan Studies explains its objectives as "To encourage traits of observation, creativity, analysis and reflection in students" (NCPS, 2006, p. 1). Furthermore, published studies provide evidence of different subjects which are used for the CT skills development such as English (Bevan, 2017; Rashid & Qaisar, 2016); English, Urdu, Islamiyat, Social Studies, etc. (Inamullah et al., 2016), Chemistry (Santos, 2017), Science and Technology (Duran & Dökme, 2016).

This thesis consisted of a qualitative study with multiple case study design. This design was considered the most relevant for the current research. Compelling and robust evidence was obtained rather what would be revealed from a single case study (Yin, 2018). Further, qualitative studies may also be conducted through different designs to fulfil the requirement of the objectives of the study. For example, in a previous study by Bevan (2017), the focus was on teachers and students' regarding CT. In this study methodology of ethnography with grounded theory was used in data collection and analysis.

Further studies may be conducted with experimental research regarding different pedagogical practices for the development and impact of students' CT skills. There are various studies in this regard, for example, impact of guided inquiry methods on CT of high school students (Azizmalayeri et al., 2012), effect of cooperative learning on students' CT (Nezami et al., 2013), effect of inquiry-based learning approach on students' CT skills (Duran & Dökme, 2016), effect of debate competition on students' CT (Othman et al., 2015), relationship of asking questions with students' CT skills development (Santos, 2017) and effect of cooperative learning on concept mapping and CT (Huang et al., 2017).

The study used qualitative data collection methods such as education policy documents analysis, semi-structured interviews and classroom observations. Future researchers may conduct studies with different quantitative methods of data collection. For example, previous studies have been conducted through different methods like questionnaire was used in various studies (Agustini & Suyatna, 2018; Bevan, 2017; Khan, 2017; Rashid & Qaisar, 2016). A recent study by Awan et al. (2018) analysed four curriculum documents for the development of CT skills in citizenship education. Four textbooks of English, Urdu, Pakistan studies and Islamiyat from secondary level were analysed with analysis of NEP (2009). Questionnaires were used to get their perceptions of the teachers. Similarly, a study conducted by Khan (2017) used a mixed-method approach with data collection methods like questionnaires, focus groups of teachers and students and classroom observations in both phases of the study.

This study was a snapshot concerning the analysis of education policy documents and science teachers' practices for the development of CT skills in secondary level students. Further studies may be conducted to measure students' CT skills. There are previous studies with measurement of CT skills through different tools, for example, through Halpern Critical Thinking using everyday situation and Watson-Glaser Critical Thinking Appraisal form (Bevan, 2017), Critical Thinking Skills Scale by Demir (2015), Critical thinking Test developed by Watson and Glaser (1980) (Azizmalayeri et al., 2012; Nezami et al., 2013) and 25 item questionnaire developed by Yeh (2009) (Huang et al., 2017).

Future researchers may conduct action research to improve the pedagogical practices of science teachers for the development of CT skills. Professional development (PD) sessions could be developed and offered for teachers to improve the CT skills among the students. PD sessions have been used to develop CT skills in IT students (Bailey & Mentz, 2015).

The current study focused on CT skills development at the secondary level with science teachers and students. Further studies may be conducted with different levels of students and teachers. For example, at elementary level (Huang et al., 2017), with 4th-grade students (Rashid & Qaisar, 2016), 6th-grade students (Duran & Dökme, 2016), 7th-grade students (Agustini & Suyatna, 2018), at secondary level (Azizmalayeri et al., 2012; Nezami et al., 2013), with university-level students (Bevan, 2017; Santoso et al., 2018) and BEd level students (Khan, 2017). Future researchers may conduct studies with different aspects in other provinces of Pakistan using different research methodology and a large sample size.

References

Abrami, P. C., Bernard, R. M., Borokhovski, E., Waddington, D. I., Wade, C. A., & Persson, T. (2015). Strategies for teaching students to think critically: A meta-analysis. *Review of Educational Research, 85*(2), 275-314.

Abrami, P. C., Bernard, R. M., Borokhovski, E., Wade, A., Surkes, M. A., Tamim, R., & Zhang, D. (2008). Instructional interventions affecting critical thinking skills and dispositions: A stage 1 meta-analysis. *Review of Educational Research, 78*(4), 1102-1134.

Agustini, R., & Suyatna, A. (2018). Developing inquiry-based practice equipment of heat conductivity to foster the students' critical thinking ability. *Jurnal Ilmiah Pendidikan Fisika Al-BiRuNi, 7*(1), 49-57.

Ahdhianto, E., Marsigit, H., & Nurfauzi, Y. (2020). Improving fifth-grade students' Mathematical problem-solving and critical thinking skills using problem-based learning. *Universal Journal of Educational Research, 8*(5), 2012-2021.

Al-Ahmadi, & Mahmood, F. (2008). *The development of scientific thinking with senior school physics students.* (Unpublished doctoral dissertation), University of Glasgow, Glasgow.

Al-Degether, R. (2009). *Teacher educators' opinion and knowledge about critical thinking and the methods they use to encourage critical thinking skills in five female teacher colleges in Saudi Arabia.* (Unpublished doctoral dissertation), University of Kansas, USA.

Al-Karaki, W. K. (2007). *The Effectiveness of a training program based on habits of mind in developing critical thinking of university students.* (Unpublished doctoral dissertation), Arabic University for Postgraduate Studies, Amman, Jordan.

Al-Osaimi, K., Reid, N., & Rodrigues, S. (2014). Critical thinking-can it be measured. *Journal of Science Education, 15*(1), 30-36.

Al-Qasmi, S. A. (2006). *Problem solving in biology at university level.* (Unpublished doctoral dissertation), University of Glasgow, Glasgow.

Al Heela, M. M. (2002). *Teaching methods and strategies.* . United Arab Emirates: Al-Ain, University Book House.

Alazzi, K. F. (2008). Teachers' perceptions of critical thinking: A study of Jordanian secondary school social studies teachers. *The Social Studies, 99*(6), 243-248.

Alexander, R. J. (2001). *Culture and pedagogy: International comparisons in primary education.* Oxford: Blackwell's Publishing.

Ali, A., & Buzdar, M. A. (2013). Development of reflective thinking through distance teacher education programs at AIOU Pakistan. *International Review of Research in Open and Distance Learning, 14*(3), 43-58.

Alosaimi, K. H. (2013). *The development of critical thinking skills in the sciences.* (Unpublished doctoral dissertation), University of Dundee, Dundee.

Arif, M. (2011). *Analysis of Mathematics curriculum at secondary school level in Pakistan.* (Unpublished doctoral dissertation), Foundation University, Islamabad.

Asrita, A., & Nurhilza, N. (2018). Students' critical thinking skills in group discussion: The case study of fifth grade students in Sukma Bangsa Bireuen elementary school. *Sukma: Jurnal Pendidikan, 2*(1), 67-92.

Ausubel, D. P. (1978). In defense of advance organizers: A reply to the critics. *Review of Educational Research, 48*(2), 251-257.

Awan, A. S., Perveen, M., & Abiodullah, M. (2018). An analysis of the critical thinking for citizenship education in the curriculum at secondary level. *Bulletin of Education and Research, 40*(1), 141-153.

Azizmalayeri, K., MirshahJafari, E., Sharif, M., Asgari, M., & Omidi, M. (2012). The impact of guided inquiry methods of teaching on the critical thinking of high school students. *Journal of Education and Practice, 3*(10), 42-48.

Bailey, R., & Mentz, E. (2015). IT teachers' experience of teaching–learning strategies to promote critical thinking. *Issues in Informing Science and Information Technology, 12*(1), 141-152. doi:10.28945/2257

Bailin, S. (2002). Critical thinking and science education. *Science & Education, 11*(4), 361-375.

Bazeley, P. (2013). *Qualitative data analysis: Practical strategies*. London: Sage Publications.

Bazeley, P., & Jackson, K. (2013). *Qualitative data analysis with NVivo*. London: Sage Publications.

Bell, J. (2014). *Doing Your Research Project: A guide for first-time researchers*. New York: McGraw-Hill Education

Ben-David, A., & Orion, N. (2013). Teachers' voices on integrating metacognition into science education. *International Journal of Science Education, 35*(18), 3161-3193.

Bevan, S. R. (2017). *Thinking culturally about critical thinking in Cambodia.* (Unpublished doctoral dissertation), London South Bank University, London.

Bialik, M., & Fadel, C. (2015). *Skills for the 21st century: What should students learn?* Boston, Massachusetts: Center for Curriculum Redesign

Blanchard, M. R., Southerland, S. A., Osborne, J. W., Sampson, V. D., Annetta, L. A., & Granger, E. M. (2010). Is inquiry possible in light of accountability?: A quantitative comparison of the relative effectiveness of guided inquiry and verification laboratory instruction. *Science education, 94*(4), 577-616.

Blaxter, L. (2010). *How to research.* New York: McGraw-Hill Education

Brinkmann, S., & Kvale, S. (2015). *InterViews: Learning the craft of qualitative research interviewing.* London: Sage Publications.

Brown, M. E., & Ganguly, S. (2003). *Fighting words: Language policy and ethnic relations in Asia.* Cambridge: Mit Press.

Charmaz, K. (2017). The power of constructivist grounded theory for critical inquiry. *Qualitative inquiry, 23*(1), 34-45.

Chen, D.-L. (2015). *Developing critical thinking through problem-based learning: an action research for a class of media literacy.* (Unpublished doctoral dissertation), Durham University, Durham.

Clarke, J. H. a. B., A. W. (1993). *Teaching critical thinking: Report from across the curriculum.* New York: Prentice-Hall Inc.

Cohen, L., Manion, L., & Morrison, K. (2007). *Research methods in education.* London: Routledge.

Conner, K., Coppley, A., & Furr, B. (2017). Questioning for critical thinking. *Instructional Modules for Professional learning Responding to Opportunities and Valuing Educators, 1*(1), 12-20.

Cooper, J. M. (2010). *Classroom teaching skills.* San Francisco: Cengage Learning.

Cottrell, S. (2011). *Critical thinking skills: Developing effective analysis and argument.* New York: Palcrave Magmillan.

Creswell, J. W. (2009). *Research design: Qualitative, quantitative, and mixed methods approaches*. London: Sage Publications.

Creswell, J. W. (2014). *A concise introduction to mixed methods research*. London: Sage Publications.

Creswell, J. W., & Poth, C. N. (2018). *Qualitative inquiry and research design: Choosing among five approaches*. United Kingdom: Sage publications.

Damas, M. N. (2007). *The modern strategies in teaching general science*. Amman: Dar Ghida Publishing and Distribution.

Demir, S. (2015). Perspectives of science teacher candidates regarding scientific creativity and critical thinking. *Journal of Education and Practice, 6*(17), 157-159.

Dewey, J. (2004). *Democracy and education*. Hazleton: The Pennsylvania State University.

Duran, M., & Dökme, İ. (2016). The effect of the inquiry-based learning approach on student's critical thinking skills. *Eurasia Journal of Mathematics, Science and Technology Education, 12*(12), 2887-2908.

Dwyer, C., Hogan, M. J., & Stewart, I. (2011). The promotion of critical thinking skills through argument mapping. In C. P, Horvath, & J. M. Forte (Eds.), *Critical Thinking* (pp. 1-26). New York: Nova Science Publishers.

Elbaz, F. (1981). The teacher's "practical knowledge": Report of a case study. *Curriculum inquiry, 11*(1), 43-71.

Elder, L., & Paul, R. (2019). *The thinker's guide to intellectual standards: The words that name them and the criteria that define them*. New York: Rowman & Littlefield.

Elo, S., Kääriäinen, M., Kanste, O., Pölkki, T., Utriainen, K., & Kyngäs, H. (2014).

Qualitative content analysis: A focus on trustworthiness. *SAGE open, 4*(1), 1-

10.

Ennis, R. (1991). Critical thinking: A streamlined conception. *Teaching Philosophy,*

14(1), 5-24.

Ennis, R. (1993). Critical thinking assessment. *Theory into practice, 32*(3), 179-186.

doi:10.1080/00405849309543594

Ennis, R. (2001). Argument appraisal strategy. *A comprehensive approach. Informal*

Logic, 21(2), 97-140.

Ennis, R. (2018). Critical thinking across the curriculum: A vision. *Topoi, 37*(1), 165-

184.

Facione, P. (1990). *The complete American Philosophical Association delphi*

research report. USA: The California Academic Press.

Facione, P. (2007). Talking critical thinking. *Change: The magazine of higher*

learning, 39(2), 38-45. doi:10.3200/CHNG.39.2.38-45

Fahim, M., & Pezeshki, M. (2012). Manipulating critical thinking skills in test taking.

International Journal of Education, 4(1), 153-160. doi:10.5296/ije.v4i1.1169

Fisher, A. (2011). *Critical thinking: An introduction.* London: Cambridge University

Press.

Fives, H., & Gill, M. G. (2014). *International handbook of research on teachers'*

beliefs. New York: Routledge.

Fung, D. (2014). Promoting critical thinking through effective group work: A

teaching intervention for Hong Kong primary school students. *International*

Journal of Educational Research, 66(3), 45-62. doi:10.1016/j.ijer.2014.02.002

Galton, M. J., & Simon, B. (1980). *Progress and performance in the primary classroom*. New York: Routledge.

Garner, J. K., Pugh, K., & Kaplan, A. (2016). *Museum visitor identification and engagement with science (VINES): A theory-driven process for designing transformational experiences*. Paper presented at the Annual Meeting of the American Educational Research Association, Washington DC.

Gibbons, P. (2013). *Scaffolding in the Routledge encyclopedia of second language acquisition*. London: Routledge.

Gilbert, J. K. (2006). *Science Education: Science, education, and the formal curriculum*. UK: Taylor & Francis.

Gillies, R. M., Ashman, A. F., & Terwel, J. (2008). *The teacher's role in implementing cooperative learning in the classroom: An introduction* (Vol. 7). New York: Springer.

Glaser. (1941). *An experiment in the development of critical thinking*. New York: Columbia University.

Glassner, A., & Schwarz, B. B. (2007). What stands and develops between creative and critical thinking? Argumentation? *Thinking skills and creativity, 2*(1), 10-18.

Graneheim, U. H., & Lundman, B. (2004). Qualitative content analysis in nursing research: concepts, procedures and measures to achieve trustworthiness. *Nurse education today, 24*(2), 105-112.

Grigg, L. (2019). Critical Thinking Pedagogy in the Classroom. Retrieved from https://www.uleth.ca/education/story/4082

Gutek, G. L. (2013). *Philosophical, ideological, and theoretical perspectives on education*. New York: Pearson Higher Ed.

Guttami, N. (2005). *Teaching thinking for children*. Amman: Dar Al-Fikr Printing and

    Publishing.

Hall, D. (2011). Debate: Innovative teaching to enhance critical thinking and

    communication skills in healthcare professionals. *Internet Journal of Allied*

    Health Sciences and Practice, 9(3), 1-7.

Halpern, D. F. (1997). Sex differences in intelligence: Implications for education.

    American Psychologist, 52(10), 1091-1105.

Halpern, D. F. (2007). The nature and nurture of critical thinking. *Critical thinking in*

    psychology, 1(1), 1-14.

Halpern, D. F. (2014). *Thought and knowledge: An introduction to critical thinking*.

    New York: Psychology Press.

Halx, M. D., & Reybold, L. E. (2006). A pedagogy of force: Faculty perspectives of

    critical thinking capacity in undergraduate students. *The Journal of General*

    Education, 54(4), 293-315. doi:10.1353/jge.2006.0009

Hancock, D. R., & Algozzine, B. (2016). *Doing case study research: A practical*

    guide for beginning researchers. New York: Teachers College Press.

Hartman, H., & Sternberg, R. J. (1992). A broad BACEIS for improving thinking.

    Instructional Science, 21(5), 401-425.

Hatcher, D. L. (2006). Stand-alone versus integrated critical thinking courses. *The*

    Journal of General Education, 55(3), 247-272. doi:10.1353/jge.2007.0002

Hermans, R., van Braak, J., & Van Keer, H. (2008). Development of the beliefs about

    primary education scale: Distinguishing a developmental and transmissive

    dimension. *Teaching and teacher Education, 24*(1), 127-139.

Higgins, S. (2015). A recent history of teaching thinking. In R. Wegerif, L. Li, & J. C. Kaufman (Eds.), *The Routledge international handbook of research on teaching thinking* (pp. 19-28). London: Routledge.

Hooks, B. (2010). *Teaching critical thinking: Practical wisdom.* New York: Routlege.

Huang, M.-Y., Tu, H.-Y., Wang, W.-Y., Chen, J.-F., Yu, Y.-T., & Chou, C.-C. (2017). Effects of cooperative learning and concept mapping intervention on critical thinking and basketball skills in elementary school. *Thinking skills and creativity, 23*(1), 207-216. doi:10.1016/j.tsc.2017.01.002

Hussain, S. (2011). *The effectiveness of teaching Physics through inquiry at Secondary School Level in Pakistan.* (Unpublished doctoral dissertation), Foundation University, Islamabad.

Hwang, G.-J., & Chang, H.-F. (2011). A formative assessment-based mobile learning approach to improving the learning attitudes and achievements of students. *Computers & Education, 56*(4), 1023-1031.

Igel, C., & Urquhart, V. (2012). Generation Z, meet cooperative learning: Properly implemented cooperative learning strategies can increase student engagement and achievement. *Middle school journal, 43*(4), 16-21.

Inamullah, H. M., Bibi, W., & Irshadullah, H. (2016). An Analytical Study of Questioning Leading to Critical Thinking in Secondary Level Classrooms. *Journal of Social Sciences & Humanities, 24*(1), 1994-7046.

Jerwan, F. (2009). *Teaching thinking: Conception and application.* Amman, Jordan: Dar Alfiker.

Johnson, D. W., & Johnson, R. T. (2009). An educational psychology success story: Social interdependence theory and cooperative learning. *Educational researcher, 38*(5), 365-379.

Kennedy, M., Fisher, M. B., & Ennis, R. H. (1991). Critical thinking: Literature review and needed research. *Educational values and cognitive instruction: Implications for reform, 2*(1), 11-40.

Khan, S. I. (2017). *An investigation of the concept of critical thinking in the context of a functional English course in a BEd Degree in Pakistan.* (Unpublished doctoral dissertation), University of Glasgow, Glasgow.

Khorraminejad, M., Ashayeri, H., Abtahi, A., Mohammakhani, K., & Soleimani, N. (2020). A reflection on Socratic questioning and critical thinking in digital games. *Quarterly of Cultural Studies & Communication, 16*(61).

Khorraminejad, M., Ashayeri, H., Abtahi, A., Mohammakhani, K., & Soleimani, N. (2021). A reflection on Socratic questioning and critical thinking in digital games. *Quarterly of Cultural Studies & Communication, 16*(61). doi:https://dx.doi.org/10.22034/jcsc.2020.131584.2185

Kim, K., Sharma, P., Land, S. M., & Furlong, K. P. (2013). Effects of active learning on enhancing student critical thinking in an undergraduate general science course. *Innovative Higher Education, 38*(3), 223-235.

Kivunja, C., & Kuyini, A. B. (2017). Understanding and applying research paradigms in educational contexts. *International Journal of higher education, 6*(5), 26-41.

Kong, S. L. (2001). *Critical thinking dispositions of pre-service teachers in Singapore: A preliminary investigation.* Paper presented at the The Annual Conference of the Australian Association for Research in Education (AARE), Fremantle, Western Australia.

Korstjens, I., & Moser, A. (2018). Series: Practical guidance to qualitative research. Part 4: trustworthiness and publishing. *European Journal of General Practice, 24*(1), 120-124.

Krathwohl, D. R. (2002). A revision of Bloom's taxonomy: An overview. *Theory into practice, 41*(4), 212-218.

Kuhn, D., & Franklin, S. (2006). The second decade: What develops (and how). *Handbook of child psychology, 2*(1), 517-550.

Kules, B. (2016). Computational thinking is critical thinking: Connecting to university discourse, goals, and learning outcomes. *Proceedings of the association for information science and technology, 53*(1), 1-6.

Kumar, M., & Natarajan, U. (2007). A problem-based learning model: Showcasing an educational paradigm shift. *The Curriculum Journal, 18*(1), 89-102.

Kvale, S. (1996). *InterViews. An introduction to qualitative research writing.* Thousand Oaks: Sage Publication.

Lai, E. R. (2011). Critical thinking: A literature review. *Pearson's Research Reports, 6*(1), 40-41.

Larsson, K. (2021). On the Role of Knowledge in Critical Thinking–Using Student Essay Responses to Bring Empirical Fuel to the Debate between 'Generalists' and 'Specifists'. *Journal of Philosophy of Education, 1*(1), 1-12.

Lewis, A., & Smith, D. (1993). Defining higher order thinking. *Theory into practice, 32*(3), 131-137.

Lin, Z., Chen, M., & Ma, Y. (2010). The augmented lagrange multiplier method for exact recovery of corrupted low-rank matrices. *arXiv preprint arXiv:1009.5055, 1*(1), 1-23.

Lopman, B. A., Reacher, M. H., Vipond, I. B., Sarangi, J., & Brown, D. W. (2004). Clinical manifestation of norovirus gastroenteritis in health care settings. *Clinical Infectious Diseases, 39*(3), 318-324.

Mahmood, S. (2017). *Testing the effectiveness of a critical thinking skills intervention for initial teacher education students in Pakistan.* (Unpublished doctoral dissertation), University of Southampton, Southampton.

Manan, S., & Mehmood, T. (2015). Culture and critical thinking in classroom: Narratives from university students in Pakistan. *Asia Pacific Journal of Social Science, 1*(3), 110-134.

Mansour, N. (2009). Science teachers' beliefs and practices: Issues, implications and research agenda. *International Journal of Environmental and Science Education, 4*(1), 25-48.

Martin, D., & Ronald, B. (2015). *The Palgrave handbook of critical thinking in higher education.* New York: Springer.

Martinez, M. E. (2006). What is metacognition? *Phi delta kappan, 87*(9), 696-699.

Mayring, P. (2014). *Qualitative content analysis: theoretical foundation, basic procedures and software solution.* Klagenfurt: SSOAR.

Mendelman, L. (2007). Critical thinking and reading. *Journal of Adolescent & Adult Literacy, 51*(4), 300-302.

Merriam, S. B. (2009). *Qualitative research and case study applications in education. Revised and expanded from "Case study research in education".* San Francisco: Jossey-Bass.

Miles, M. B., Huberman, A. M., & Saldana, J. (2014). *Qualitative data analysis: A method sourcebook.* CA, US: Sage Publications.

Moon, J. A. (2008). *Critical thinking: An exploration of theory and practice*. London: Routledge.

Moseley, D., Baumfield, V., Elliott, J., Higgins, S., Newton, D. P., Miller, J., & Gregson, M. (2005). *Frameworks for thinking: A handbook for teaching and learning*. United Kindgdom: Cambridge University Press.

Mulhall, A. (2003). In the field: notes on observation in qualitative research. *Journal of advanced nursing, 41*(3), 306-313.

Muller, E. (2017). Document analysis: Comparing and contrasting the early years education of Estonia and England to highlight the similarities and differences and impact of respective countries children. *The STeP Journal, 4*(2), 95-112.

Naseer, H., Muhammad, Y., & Masood, S. (2020). Critical Thinking Skills in a Secondary School Pakistan Studies Textbook: A Qualitative Content Analysis. *Sir Syed Journal of Education & Social Research, 3*(4), 84-95.

NC. (2006). *National curriculum for grades IX-X*. Islamabad: Ministry of Education, Government of Pakistan.

NCB. (2006). *National curriculum for Biology grades IX – X*. Islamabad: Ministry of Education, Government of Pakistan.

NCC. (2006). *National curriculum for Chemistry grades IX – X*. Islamabad: Ministry of Education, Government of Pakistan.

NCE. (2006). *National curriculum for English grades IX – X*. Islamabad: Ministry of Education, Government of Pakistan.

NCP. (2006). *National curriculum for Physics grades IX – X*. Islamabad: Ministry of Education, Government of Pakistan.

NCPS. (2006). *National Curriculum for Pakistan Studies Grades IX – X*. Islamabad: Ministry of Education, Government of Pakistan.

NEP. (2009). *The National Education Policy (NEP)*. Islamabad: Ministry of Education, Government of Pakistan.

Nezami, N. R., Asgari, M., & Dinarvand, H. (2013). The effect of cooperative learning on the critical thinking of High School students. *Technical Journal of Engineering and Applied Sciences, 3*(19), 2508-2514.

Norris, S., & Ennis, R. (1989). What is critical thinking. *The practitioner's guide to teaching thinking series: Evaluating critical thinking, 1*(1), 1-26.

Nugent, P. M., & Vitale, B. A. (2008). *Fundamentals success: A course review applying critical thinking to test taking*. Philadelphia: FA Davis.

Orlich, D. C., Harder, R. J., Callahan, R. C., Trevisan, M. S., & Brown, A. H. (2012). *Teaching strategies: A guide to effective instruction*. Boston: Warsworth.

Osborne, J. (2014). Teaching critical thinking? New directions in science education. *School Science Review, 95*(352), 53-62.

Othman, M., Sahamid, H., Zulkefli, M. H., Hashim, R., & Mohamad, F. (2015). The effects of debate competition on critical thinking among Malaysian second language learners. *Middle-East Journal of Scientific Research, 23*(4), 656-664.

p21. (2007). Partnership for 21st Century Skills (P21). Framework for 21st Century Learning. Retrieved from https://www.battelleforkids.org/networks/p21/frameworks-resources

Pajares, M. F. (1992). Teachers' beliefs and educational research: Cleaning up a messy construct. *Review of Educational Research, 62*(3), 307-332.

Patton, M. Q. (2002). Designing qualitative studies. *Qualitative Research and Evaluation Methods, 3*(5), 230-246.

Patton, M. Q. (2015). *Qualitative research & research methods (4th ed.)*. Thousand Oaks: Sage Publications.

Paul, R. (1995). *Critical thinking: How to prepare students for a rapidly changing world*. Santa Rosa, CA: Foundation for Critical Thinking.

Paul, R., & Elder, L. (2006a). *Critical thinking reading & writing test*. Tomales, CA: Foundation for Critical Thinking.

Paul, R., & Elder, L. (2006b). Critical thinking: The nature of critical and creative thought. *Journal of Developmental Education, 30*(2), 1-34.

Paul, R., & Elder, L. (2006c). *The thinker's guide to scientific thinking*. Tomales, CA: Foundation for Critical Thinking.

Paul, R., Elder, L., & Bartell, T. (1997). *California teacher preparation for instruction in critical thinking: Research findings and policy recommendations*. Clifornia: California Commission on Teacher Credentialing, Sacramento.

Phan, H. P. (2008). Achievement goals, the classroom environment, and reflective thinking: A conceptual framework. *Electronic Journal of Research in Educational Psychology, 6*(3), 571-602.

Phonna, D., Safitri, R., & Syukri, M. (2021). *Guided inquiry-based on practicum to improve critical thinking skills on the subject of Newton's law*. Paper presented at the Journal of Physics: Conference Series, Orlando, Fl.

Piper, H., & Simons, H. (2005). Research methods in the social sciences. In B. Somekh & C. Lewin (Eds.), (pp. 56-63). London: Sage Publications.

Pithers, R. T., & Soden, R. (2000). Critical thinking in education: A review. *Educational Research, 42*(3), 237-249.

Poulson, L., Avramidis, E., Fox, R., Medwell, J., & Wary, D. (2001). The theoretical orientation of primary school literacy teachers: An exploratory study. *Research Papers in Education, 16*(3), 271-292.

Rahman, T. (2005). Passports to privilege: The English-medium schools in Pakistan. *Peace and Democracy in South Asia, 1*(1), 24-44.

Rahmatih, A., Indraswati, D., Gunawan, G., Widodo, A., Maulyda, M., & Erfan, M. (2021). *An Analysis of Questioning Skill in Elementary School Pre-service Teachers Based on Bloom's Taxonomy.* Paper presented at the Journal of Physics: Conference Series, Orlando, Fl.

Ramnarain, U. (2011). Teachers' use of questioning in supporting learners doing science investigations. *South African Journal of Education, 31*(1), 91-101.

Ramos, J. L. S., Dolipas, B. B., & Villamor, B. B. (2013). Higher order thinking skills and academic performance in physics of college students: A regression analysis. *International Journal of Innovative Interdisciplinary Research, 1*(4), 48-60.

Rashid, S., & Qaisar, S. (2016). Developing Critical Thinking through Questioning Strategy among Fourth Grade Students. *Bulletin of Education and Research, 38*(2), 153-168.

Rehman, F. (2004). *Analysis of National science curriculum (chemistry) at secondary level in Pakistan.* (Unpublished doctoral dissertation), University of Arid Agriculture, Rawalpindi.

Richardson, V. (2003). Constructivist pedagogy. *Teachers college record, 105*(9), 1623-1640.

Rind, A. A., & Mughal, S. H. (2020). An Analysis of Pakistan's National Curriculum of Mathematics at Secondary level. *Electronic Journal of Education, Social Economics and Technology, 1*(1), 39-42.

Rossi, I. V., de Lima, J. D., Sabatke, B., Nunes, M. A. F., Ramirez, G. E., & Ramirez, M. I. (2020). Active learning tools improve the learning outcomes, scientific attitude and critical thinking in higher education: Experiences in an online course during the COVID-19 pandemic. *bioRxiv*. doi:https://doi.org/10.1101/2020.12.22.423922

Royhana, U., Sumiharsono, R., & Septory, B. (2021). *Analysis of students' mathematical critical thinking ability on the problem of algebraic factorization and implementation of cooperative learning in the type of student teams achievement divisions to improve students' critical thinking ability.* Paper presented at the Journal of Physics: Conference Series, Orlando.

Saeed, T., Khan, S., Ahmed, A., Gul, R., Cassum, S., & Parpio, Y. (2012). Development of students' critical thinking: the educators' ability to use questioning skills in the baccalaureate programmes in nursing in Pakistan. *Journal of the Pakistan Medical Association, 62*(3), 200-203.

Santos, L. F. (2017). The role of critical thinking in science education. *Journal of Education and Practice, 8*(20), 159-173.

Santoso, T., Yuanita, L., & Erman, E. (2018). *The role of student's critical asking question in developing student's critical thinking skills.* Paper presented at the Journal of Physics: Conference Series.

Savich, C. (2009). Improving Critical Thinking Skills in History. *Networks: An Online Journal for Teacher Research, 11*(2), 1-13. doi:10.4148/2470-6353.1106

Schiro, M. S. (2012). *Curriculum theory: Conflicting visions and enduring concerns* (2nd ed.). New York: Sage Publications, Inc.

Schraw, G., Crippen, K. J., & Hartley, K. (2006). Promoting self-regulation in science education: Metacognition as part of a broader perspective on learning. *Research in Science Education, 36*(1-2), 111-139.

Schreier, M. (2012). *Qualitative content analysis in practice*. London: Sage

Publications.

Schwartz-Shea, P., & Yanow, D. (2013). *Interpretive research design: Concepts and*

processes. London: Routledge.

Shulman, L. S. (1986). Those who understand: Knowledge growth in teaching.

Educational researcher, 15(2), 4-14.

Simpson, M., & Tuson, J. (2003). *Using observations in small-scale research: A*

beginner's guide. Revised edition. Using research. Scotland: The SCRE

Centre.

Siraj-Blatchford, I., Muttock, S., Sylva, K., Gilden, R., & Bell, D. (2002).

Researching effective pedagogy in the early years. Norwich: Department of

Education and Skills.

Snyder, L. G., & Snyder, M. J. (2008). Teaching critical thinking and problem solving

skills. *The Journal of Research in Business Education, 50*(2), 90-100.

Spatariu, A., Winsor, D. L., Simpson, C., & Hosman, E. (2016). Further classification

and methodological considerations of evaluations for online discussion in

instructional settings. *Turkish Online Journal of Educational Technology-*

TOJET, 15(1), 43-52.

Sternberg, R. J. (1986). *Criticial thinking: Its nature, measurement, and improvement*.

New Haven, CT: Yale University.

Sutiani, A., Situmorang, M., & Silalahi, A. (2021). Implementation of an Inquiry

Learning Model with Science Literacy to Improve Student Critical Thinking

Skills. *International Journal of Instruction, 14*(2), 117-138.

Swartz, R. (2003). Infusing critical and creative thinking into instruction. In D.Fasko

    (Ed.), *Critical Thinking and Reasoning: Current Research, Theory and*

    Practice (pp. 207-251). Cresskill NJ: Hampton Press.

Theobald, P. (2009). *Education Now: How Re-thinking America's Past Can Change*

    Its Future. Colorado: Paradigm.

Ting, M., & Abdullah, M. S. H. B. (2020). Cooperative learning foster critical

    thinking in mainland China: a review. *EurAsian Journal of BioSciences, 14*(1),

    5975-5979.

Tok, E. (2012). The opinions of preschool teacher candidates about creative thinking.

    Procedia-Social and Behavioral Sciences, 47(1), 1523-1528.

    doi:10.1016/j.sbspro.2012.06.854

Tsai, C.-C. (2001). A review and discussion of epistemological commitments,

    metacognition, and critical thinking with suggestions on their enhancement in

    Internet-assisted chemistry classrooms. *Journal of Chemical Education, 78*(7),

    970-982.

Tsay, M., & Brady, M. (2010). A case study of cooperative learning and

    communication pedagogy: Does working in teams make a difference? *Journal*

    of the Scholarship of Teaching and Learning, 10(2), 78-89.

Tseng, C.-H., Tuan, H.-L., & Chin, C.-C. (2013). How to help teachers develop

    inquiry teaching: Perspectives from experienced science teachers. *Research in*

    Science Education, 43(2), 809-825.

Tsui, L. (2002). Fostering critical thinking through effective pedagogy: Evidence

    from four institutional case studies. *The Journal of Higher Education, 73*(6),

    740-763.

Turner, J. C. (1995). The influence of classroom contexts on young children's motivation for literacy. *Reading Research Quarterly, 1*(1), 410-441.

Turuk, M. C. (2008). The relevance and implications of Vygotsky's sociocultural theory in the second language classroom. *Arecls, 5*(1), 244-262.

Udall, A. J., & Daniels, J. E. (1991). *Creating the Thoughtful Classroom: Strategies To Promote Student Thinking. Grades (3-12)*. Tucson: Zephyr Press.

Vieira, R. M., Tenreiro-Vieira, C., & Martins, I. P. (2011). Critical thinking: Conceptual clarification and its importance in science education. *Science Education International, 22*(1), 43-54.

Vygotsky, L. S. (1980). *Mind in society: The development of higher psychological processes*. Cambridge, MA: Harvard university press.

Wagner, T. (2014). *The global achievement gap: Why even our best schools don't teach the new survival skills our children need and what we can do about it:* . New York: Basic Books.

Wahyuni, S., Qamariah, H., Syahputra, M., Yusuf, Y. Q., & Ganin, S. A. (2020). Challenges and solutions to develop critical thinking with the British Parliamentary Debate System in EFL classrooms. *International Journal of Language Studies, 14*(3), 137-156.

Watson, G. (1980). *Watson-Glaser Critical Thinking Appraisal*. San Antonio: Psychological Corporation

Wilkening, F., & Sodian, B. (2005). Scientific reasoning in young children: Introduction. *Swiss Journal of Psycholog, 64*(3), 137-139.

Willingham, D. T. (2009). *Why don't students like school?: A cognitive scientist answers questions about how the mind works and what it means for the classroom*. United States: John Wiley & Sons.

Willingham, D. T. (2019). How to teach critical thinking. *Education: Future Frontiers, 1*(1), 1-17.

Woolfolk, A. E. (2004). *Educational Psychology*. Singapore: Person Education, Inc.

Yacoubian, H. A. (2015). A framework for guiding future citizens to think critically about nature of science and socioscientific issues. *Canadian Journal of Science, Mathematics and Technology Education, 15*(3), 248-260. doi:10.1080/14926156.2015.1051671

Yang, Y.-T. C., Newby, T. J., & Bill, R. L. (2005). Using Socratic questioning to promote critical thinking skills through asynchronous discussion forums in distance learning environments. *The American Journal of Distance Education, 19*(3), 163-181.

Yazan, B. (2015). Three approaches to case study methods in education: Yin, Merriam, and Stake. *The Qualitative Report, 20*(2), 134-152.

Yeh, Y.-C. (2009). Integrating e-learning into the Direct-instruction Model to enhance the effectiveness of critical-thinking instruction. *Instructional Science, 37*(2), 185-203.

Yin, R. K. (2013). Validity and generalization in future case study evaluations. *Evaluation, 19*(3), 321-332.

Yin, R. K. (2014). *Case study research: Design and methods (5th ed.)*. New York: Sage publications.

Yin, R. K. (2018). *Case study research and applications: Design and methods*. New York: Sage publications.

Youngblood, N., & Beitz, J. (2001). Developing critical thinking with active learning strategies. . *Nurse Educator, 26*(1), 39-42.

Yuliawati, Y., Mahmud, M., & Muliati, M. (2016). Teacher's questioning and

students' critical thinking in EFL classroom interaction. *ELT WORLDWIDE,*

3(2), 231-247.

Zhang, L., & Kim, S. (2018). Critical thinking cultivation in Chinese college English

classes. *English Language Teaching, 11*(8), 1-6.

Zhao, C., Pandian, A., & Singh, M. K. M. (2016). Instructional Strategies for

Developing Critical Thinking in EFL Classrooms. *English Language*

Teaching, 9(10), 14-21.

Zikmund, W. G., Babin, B. J., Carr, J. C., & Griffin, M. (2013). *Business research*

methods. Mason, USA: Cengage Learning.

An Analysis of Education Policy Documents and Science Teachers' Practices for Developing Critical Thinking Skills in Secondary School Students

Appendix A: Interview Guide

Demographic Information of the Participant

Name of Teacher: _______________________   Name of School: _______________

Qualification: (Academic & Professional: _____________________Age: _____ (Years)

Teaching Experience: __________________Teaching Subject: _______________

1. Perception about the concept of "Critical Thinking"

1. Are you familiar with the concept of "critical thinking" and critical thinking (hereafter CT) skills? Explain your answer with examples please.

2. Importance of CT

2. In your perception, what is the importance of CT in improving quality education? Elaborate your answer with examples.

3. What do you think about importance of CT in science subjects? Explain your answer with its different aspects.

4. Do you think there is need to develop CT skills in secondary school science students? If yes, then how can CT skills be developed while teaching science subjects? Provide your answer with examples?

3. Focus/Encouragement & Training by Education Department for CT

skills development

5. What do you perceive about the importance of CT skills development in National Education policies and curriculum documents for science subjects?

6. In your opinion, what is the focus of the education department about CT skills development? Explain in the view of your experience regarding visits/ monitoring of educational offices.

7. Do your educational officers/inspectors ever encourage/motivate you to develop CT skills in science students?

8. Have you received any stuff/ printing material from education department to develop CT skills among secondary school science students? If yes how do you use in your practice?

9. Have you participated in any training/ professional development or refresher course regarding teaching methods/techniques for the development of CT skills? Explain your answer keeping in view your past experience.

4. Pedagogical Practice used by Teachers in classroom

10. What do you know about pedagogy and pedagogical practices/ teaching methods which are used during the science teaching? Elaborate your answer with examples.

11. Do you use student-centred/ participative/ interactive teaching methods? If yes, then explain with examples in the view of your personal experience of the classroom.

12. What is your perception about the use of cooperative learning/ group work methods in your science class room? If yes, explain with examples how these are helpful in developing CT skills in science students.

13. Do you use questioning/ inquiry based teaching/ learning methods while teaching your science subject? If yes, explain your answer with examples how is it beneficial in promoting CT skills among secondary school students?

14. What do you think about discussion/ debates/ dialogue techniques to be used in the classroom for the development of CT skills? Elaborate the answer with your personal experience.

15. Do you use activity based/ practical/ demonstration methods during teaching your science subject? If yes, explain with examples how is it beneficial in developing CT skills among science students?

16. What is your perception about the use of problem solving techniques for the development of CT skills? Explain according to your previous experience.

17. Do you use Audio-visual aids (white-board, charts, models, flowcharts, diagrams) for CT skills development in science students? Explain your answer from your personal classroom experience.

18. Which type of teaching strategies/ methods do you use for teaching science? What is the main focus of your teaching? Explain with your personal experience.

19. Do you encourage/ motivate your students regarding the development of CT skills in them? Explain your answer with your previous experience.

5. Assessment system regarding CT skills development and Suggestions

20. What do you think about the current assessment/ exam system of Board of Intermediate and Secondary Education (BISE) regarding developing CT skills in science students'? Elaborate with your personal experience.

21. How assessment system can be revised for developing CT skills among secondary school science students? What do you suggest in this regard?

6. Barriers/ Hurdles in developing CT skills

22. What problems/ barriers/ hurdles do you face regarding development of CT skills in science students? Explain in the view of your previous experience.

23. Do you think there should be in-service teacher training/ refresher? course for science teachers to develop CT skills in science students?

24. What strategies/ implications would you like to suggest/ recommend for the development of CT skills among secondary level science students?

25. Furthermore, what will you want to say about the development of CT skills in science students?